THE CHIEF FINANCIAL OFFICER

OTHER ECONOMIST BOOKS

Guide to Analysing Companies
Guide to Business Modelling
Guide to Business Planning
Guide to Cash Management
Guide to Commodities
Guide to Decision Making
Guide to Economic Indicators
Guide to Emerging Markets
Guide to the European Union
Guide to Financial Management
Guide to Financial Markets
Guide to Hedge Funds
Guide to Investment Strategy
Guide to Management Ideas and Gurus
Guide to Managing Growth
Guide to Organisation Design
Guide to Project Management
Guide to Supply Chain Management
Numbers Guide
Style Guide

Book of Business Quotations
Book of Isms
Book of Obituaries
Brands and Branding
Business Consulting
Business Strategy
Buying Professional Services
Doing Business in China
Economics
Managing Talent
Managing Uncertainty
Marketing
Marketing for Growth
Megachange – the world in 2050
Modern Warfare, Intelligence and Deterrence
Organisation Culture
Successful Strategy Execution
The World of Business

Directors: an A–Z Guide
Economics: an A–Z Guide
Investment: an A–Z Guide
Negotiation: an A–Z Guide

Pocket World in Figures

THE CHIEF FINANCIAL OFFICER

What CFOs do, the influence they have, and why it matters

What CFOs do, the influence they have, and why it matters

Jason Karaian

PUBLICAFFAIRS
New York

To Leo and Harriet, a top executive team

Contents

Acknowledgements

IN THE COURSE OF REPORTING for this book, I was struck by how often a CFO I spoke to one day became a CEO the next. Or a chairman. Or moved to a different company, in a different country, in a different industry.

Belying its somewhat staid image, the world of the CFO is in constant flux. For this reason, I am grateful to the many finance chiefs who generously gave me their time and put up with my questions; most of them are cited in the text by name.

Special thanks also to Janet Kersnar for her insightful comments on draft chapters and, in general, for passing on her extensive knowledge of the subject. Marie Leone, Barney Southin and Chen Wu went out of their way to help me at various stages of the writing process. Thank you to Daniel Franklin for the introduction and Elizabeth Bramson-Boudreau for the time to delve into this project. At Profile Books, thanks to Stephen Brough for encouragement and to Paul Lewis and Penny Williams for skilful direction and editing.

Most of all, thanks to Daianna: editor, researcher, motivator and much else besides. I could not wish for a better partner, in books and in life.

Jason Karaian
January 2014

Introduction

STRATEGIC PARTNER. Trusted adviser. Devil's advocate. There is no single way to describe the role of the chief financial officer. CFOs themselves struggle to provide an answer.[1] What is agreed, however, is that the dismissive stereotype of a mere book-keeper or bean counter no longer applies.

The CFO is the head of the finance department, of course, but in practice this is an excessively narrow view of the role's responsibilities. Only the chief executive wields as much influence within a company. Other functional executives, like the heads of marketing, technology or human resources, do not come close. The heads of regional or divisional business units may sit at the same level in the corporate hierarchy as the CFO, but their remits are more limited in scope.

This book explains who CFOs are, what they do, and why it matters. It details how finance chiefs earned their privileged position and what the future may hold for them. It describes their ever-expanding role, and how they are transforming their departments and revamping their teams to deal with this growing complexity. It examines the relationships that CFOs must forge, both inside and outside their companies, to achieve their goals.

This is intended as a reference for current finance chiefs to enable them to learn the latest thinking from their peers and benchmark their own performance; those looking to build a career in corporate finance; non-financial executives seeking to improve their relationship with the finance department; and service providers – banks and accounting and consulting firms, among others – that want to get on the good side of the keeper of the corporate chequebook. Many outside the finance department still find it difficult to relate to modern finance chiefs, as outdated notions of their remit persist. To this end, it is crucial to understand their origins, motivations and pressures.

Cash is king

Years ago, when new writers joined the staff of CFO magazine – as the author of this book once did – they were given a dog-eared memo about how to write for the publication. It included a flippant, but accurate, summary of the roots of the CFO role:

> In the beginning, there was cash. Soon, an owner put the cash to work and sought a return. Eventually, keeping tabs on the money seemed like a good idea but the owner had other priorities, namely, finding more ways to make money. Someone was needed to make sure that the owner received his or her due while paying attention to other matters, and the finance profession was born. Since that time, companies have centralised and decentralised, merged and splurged, but fundamentals remain the same. Hence, the finance exec's hoary dictum: "Show me the money, because I must show it to the owner."

From the pervasive influence of financial markets to the growth of data-driven decision-making, at each step in the evolution of the modern corporation the CFO's skill set has proved uniquely in tune with the times. This suggests that the finance chief's time in the spotlight will endure.

As guardian of the balance sheet, the CFO must be convinced that the numbers in a business case pass muster before putting it into action. A major technology purchase may thrill the IT department, or a new promotional campaign seem like a no-brainer to marketing, but these initiatives will falter if they fail to find favour with the CFO. Anyone selling big-ticket products or services to companies also needs to understand the CFO's pressures and priorities to stand a chance of winning contracts.

Successful executive teams are often marked by a healthy tension between a bullish, hard-charging CEO and a cautious, independent-minded CFO. Few senior executives other than the CFO are expected, or even encouraged, to challenge the boss as part of their daily routines. Investors looking for guidance on a company's plans often prefer to quiz straight-talking CFOs instead of cheerleading CEOs. CFOs also benefit from extensive time spent with the board of directors, giving them access and input into a company's strategic plans.

The irony of the CFO's lofty status and far-reaching influence is that the finance department does not itself command vast resources. In fact, the finance function is subject to relentless pressure to cut costs – and since CFOs often ask others to trim their budgets, this is a sensible way to set the example of a lean and efficient department (to eat their own cooking, as it were).

All guts no glory

As the de facto second-in-command charged with enforcing discipline and controls, CFO can sometimes be a lonely position. When a company is performing well the CEO often gets fawning media coverage while the CFO gets analysts and investors grumbling about why it isn't doing even better. "The CFO of a well-run company gets all of the guts but none of the glory," said Alvaro de Molina, following his departure as finance chief of Bank of America.

This may be so, but it depends on the CFO's outlook. One finance chief says that half of his counterparts are "frustrated financial controllers", struggling with the multifaceted demands that companies now place on CFOs. The other half, by contrast, comprises "wannabe chief executives" who revel in the responsibility and aim for an even higher corporate station. (He is in the latter camp, he says.)

The breadth of experience that CFOs gain on their way to the top makes them an increasingly sought after commodity. More than half of externally recruited CFOs at the largest companies in the United States are appointed from a company in a different industry, a sign of their versatility. Only a quarter of CEOs appointed from the outside are poached from a different sector. The number of CFOs promoted to CEO continues to rise, often after a rotation through a regional or divisional general manager position. Former finance chiefs are also fixtures in many boardrooms as non-executive directors.

And so the odds that a senior executive spent time in the finance function on the way up the corporate ladder are rising. Thus the CFO's methodical, data-driven approach to decision-making is gaining proponents over the archaic "gut feel" school of management. "Number cruncher" was once considered an insult, but as the volume and velocity of data expand exponentially it is becoming a badge of honour, as companies seeking to harness the insights within the data will inevitably turn to their CFOs for guidance, boosting their status even further.

But it is best to start at the beginning. A discussion of the origins of the modern CFO role is the subject of Chapter 1.

Throughout this book, chief financial officer, or CFO, is used to identify the most senior executive with responsibility for a company's finance function. In the UK, this person is often called the finance director, which in other countries sometimes confusingly applies to more junior financial staff. In continental Europe and Japan, the top finance role often carries a generic title like senior vice-president, executive vice-president or member of the management board. Other regional variations abound. Whatever the case, the CFO is almost always a member of the executive committee, if not the full board of directors.

1 Origins: from the back office to the front line

IN 1962, the Controllers Institute of America changed its name to the Financial Executives Institute. This otherwise mundane rebranding of a professional association marked a significant turning point in the status of the chief financial officer. Around this time, the CFO title began to appear formally on business cards and office doors, establishing a new tier of seniority above the long-established roles of controller, treasurer or vice-president of finance.[1] This acknowledged the larger strategic role that the head of the finance department was gaining in boardrooms across the country.

The trend began around the turn of the 20th century, when the first recognisable precursors to modern financial managers saw their influence extend beyond a narrow accounting remit. In a 1924 book about municipal finance in the UK, the treasurer of the borough of Blackpool considered the statutory duties of the county finance chief "meagre and unsatisfactory, while his actual responsibilities are heavy and important". The title of treasurer, "although euphonious, is out of harmony with his multifarious duties," he argued, suggesting variations of "controller" or even "director" as a better name for the manager whose role went well beyond a mere "custodian of cash".

Variations on this theme crop up time and again throughout the history of the modern financial executive. For more than a century, the role of the CFO has experienced perpetual reinvention. Thanks to both cyclical and secular factors, the CFO's skills have proved to be in tune with broader economic trends. At each new stage of development, the inevitable upshot is a broader role for the corporate finance chief.

The early years

In the second half of the 19th century, accounting was established as a chartered, certified profession in the UK, the United States and elsewhere in the West.[2] Accountants who worked for a single company, rather than on behalf of multiple clients at a public practice, were not as conspicuous or organised until the early 20th century. Only a handful of private industrial firms in the United States employed a controller before 1900, with General Electric believed to be among the first. A mere 1% of the membership of the Institute of Chartered Accountants in England and Wales – one of the world's oldest professional accountancy bodies, founded in 1880 – was employed by industry in 1911.

The growing ranks of corporate accountants, commonly known as controllers (or sometimes comptrollers), began to form their own associations. In the UK, the Institute of Cost and Works Accountants was formed in 1919 to serve the specific needs of corporate finance managers. The Controllers Institute of America was founded in New York in 1931. By the end of the 1960s, similar professional groups were established in Australia, Canada, France, Germany, Italy and Mexico, among others.

The executives in these pioneering groups rose to prominence thanks to the increasingly sophisticated methods they devised to evaluate and monitor financial performance. These analytical innovations changed the way companies thought about strategy, boosting the role of finance – and, by extension, the CFO – in the process.

DuPont is an example. Pierre du Pont, along with two cousins, took control of the family firm in 1902, then a manufacturer of explosives. The new owners streamlined the group into three operating units and centralised the sales and finance departments. This consolidation resulted in the number of staff in the finance function, which Pierre du Pont ran, growing from a dozen in 1903 to more than 200 a year later.

Along with protégés John Raskob and Donaldson Brown, Pierre du Pont helped develop the concept of return on investment, giving the company a better understanding of the profitability of its various product lines. The prevailing practice at the time featured rudimentary measures of profit based largely on comparing sales with direct operating costs and the replacement value of equipment. By compiling a more comprehensive schedule of direct and indirect costs, including head-office overheads, working capital and, crucially, invested capital, DuPont's finance department provided management with finely tuned measures of the rates of return generated by each business line. The contribution of individual departments in the production process – manufacturing, administration, sales and transport – were also now apparent.

When DuPont built a stake in the then-ailing General Motors, Pierre du Pont, by then president of the eponymous firm, dispatched Raskob and Brown to apply similar methods at the automaker. Brown, in particular, is credited with a number of important refinements in financial analysis, planning and budgeting practices; as GM's head of finance from the mid-1920s, he and the chief executive, Alfred Sloan, oversaw years of rapid growth at the company, which soon became the world's largest. As Alfred Chandler, a business historian, put it:

> With these innovations, modern managers had completed the essential tools by which the visible hand of management was able to replace the invisible hand of market forces in co-ordinating and monitoring economic activities.

By applying a systematic, financial lens to business operations, CFOs steadily gained a stronger hand in steering company strategy. As companies grew larger, more complex and diversified, financial measures proved ideal in assessing performance from the distant perch of the corporate headquarters.

This abstract, accounting-driven perspective drew criticism from some corners, feeding stereotypes of the penny-pinching, numbers-obsessed CFO. Playing to type, within six months of its founding, the Controllers Institute's records show that the directors found costs to cut, trimming the organisation's budget for telephone calls, water and ice. In a speech to the institute in 1932, Thomas Watson, then president of IBM, urged the audience to take responsibility "not only for conserving funds and other assets, but also for inaugurating expenditures that will make profits". The tension between conservatism and control, on one hand, and partnering with colleagues to promote growth on the other, remains a theme for CFOs to the present day.

The notion of the finance chief as striving to be more than a scorekeeper – less charitably, a bean counter – has a long historical precedent. Paul Urquhart, finance chief of the Aluminum Company of America, said in 1936 that he considered the controller "not a production manager of figures but a sales manager of ideas". In 1951, H.E. Humphreys, president of the United States Rubber Company, stressed that controllers were not "cold customers with comptometers for heads and double-entry ledgers where their hearts should be". Similar assertions continue to be made today, suggesting that not all finance chiefs have completely dispelled the old stereotypes.

Rise of conglomerates

Armed with new analytical tools, finance chiefs came into their own in the 1950s and 1960s, when the fashion for sprawling conglomerates reached its peak. Stricter anti-monopoly regulations, particularly in the United States, discouraged concentration in a single industry; growth-minded managers were thus encouraged to expand into unrelated areas in search of profits. Financial criteria served as the benchmark by which business units – regardless of their unique characteristics and circumstances – were measured, since top executives could not claim to have experience in all of the areas in which these groups operated. As Neil Fligstein, a sociologist at the University of California, Berkeley, explains in his book *The Transformation of Corporate Control*:

> From the finance perspective, the firm was a collection of assets earning varying rates of return. The firm's central goal was to allocate capital across product lines in order to increase short-term rates of return ... The finance conception of control viewed the central office as a bank and treated the divisions as potential borrowers.

By the mid-1950s, General Electric boasted more than 100 operating divisions. Other diversified conglomerates like ITT and Textron in the United States, Hanson, Saint-Gobain and Veba in Europe, and the *keiretsu* business groups in Japan were also busy bulking up around this time. In a 1963 speech, Stanley Harding, deputy controller at Shell, an Anglo-Dutch oil company, described the central role that finance played in steering company strategy:

> No well-managed business of size is today managed "by ear" and finance is the focal point, where management's flair and sense of judgment can be confirmed against facts and forecasts based upon sound controls and information.

The primacy of finance was indeed evident in the boardroom. In the United States, company presidents with backgrounds in manufacturing and sales gave way to those with finance experience. According to Fligstein, the share of presidents with a finance background at the 100 largest companies rose to 22% at the end of the 1960s, double the percentage 20 years earlier. Notable finance chiefs promoted to the chief executive role at this time included Gerald Phillippe at General Electric, Lynn Townsend at Chrysler and Alexander Galloway at RJ Reynolds.

Harold Geneen, an accountant, gained recognition for boosting the fortunes of various industrial groups by introducing intricate control systems and sophisticated processes of financial analysis. After rising to executive vice-president at Raytheon, a US defence company, he was tapped as president of ITT in 1959. During his tenure at ITT, which lasted until 1977, he oversaw more than 350 acquisitions and boosted revenues from less than $1 billion to a peak of $17 billion. By the end of the 1970s, finance had surpassed manufacturing as the most common origin for chief executives at the country's largest corporations.

As the benign economic conditions of the post-war period gave way to stagnation and inflation in the 1970s, finance chiefs were called on to prove their worth in a more defensive capacity. With growth in short supply, firms were forced to rely on internal cash flow, instead of acquisitions or external borrowing, much more than before. This forced "drastic changes in role and operating style on the chief financial officer", according to a 1976 article in *Harvard Business Review*, written by two McKinsey consultants, one of whom, Louis Gerstner, would go on to run IBM, saving the computer-maker from bankruptcy in the early 1990s.

Having gained prominence for their skills in evaluating large portfolios of businesses, CFOs now faced grittier, operational challenges. Instead of assessing a business unit's performance from afar, finance chiefs were charged with employing their talents on the front lines, as the McKinsey consultants explained:

> In most of the companies that have most successfully weathered the change of economic climate, the financial officer's response to this challenge has been vigorous and direct; he is down in the trenches, battling it out as part of the operating team. (In some cases, he's driving the team.)

This foretold the business-partnering role that would become a principal facet of the CFO role. The benefits of a dose of financial engineering to an underperforming business would soon become apparent in a big way, as the influence of capital markets began to be felt more sharply.

Marketmakers

As the nascent market for high-yield debt – otherwise known as "junk" bonds – boomed in the 1980s, companies took advantage of this new source of finance to load up on leverage. The internal capital markets of cash-rich conglomerates – where losses at one unit could be funded with the profits from another – made way for deeper pools of funds financed by external investors. This left less room for slack; meeting interest payments created a new urgency for CFOs to monitor the financial health of their firms more closely.

At the same time, the greater availability of debt encouraged a new breed of investor to take aim at the conglomerates hobbled by difficult economic conditions. Private equity firms raised mountains of debt to seize control of companies they considered undervalued. Adjusted for inflation, the leveraged buy-out of RJR Nabisco by KKR in 1989, worth $31 billion at the time, remains the largest private equity deal in history.

The tide was turning against the conglomerate model, with notions of "core competence" ascendant. To this end, private equity-owned companies ruthlessly cut costs, divested assets and streamlined operations. In striving to service the large debts taken out with creditors and extract large dividends for themselves, the new owners managed cash flows like hawks. To fend off potential private equity takeovers, other companies took pre-emptive action to slim down and boost efficiency. Either way, the onus was on CFOs to revamp their companies both financially and operationally. The skills and knowledge they gained from building up diversified conglomerates came in handy when deciding how best to dismantle them.

Pressures were also building in a different corner of the capital markets. For many years, companies with stockmarket listings sought to meet investors' expectations by growing earnings. It was a rather clubby world, with key investors' identities and motivations easily defined. As a result, the burden of serving and communicating with shareholders was manageable, and penalties for profit shortfalls were modest. Starting in the 1980s, share registers were transformed, and by the mid-1990s sophisticated institutional investors represented the majority of shareholders at most large firms.

As with the junk-bond boom of the 1980s, in the 1990s companies rushed to raise equity capital while the going was good; initial public offerings on US exchanges in the five years to 2000 were worth as much as listings in the previous 25 years combined. The demand for professional equity research grew as a result, fostering a much larger class of analysts that companies now needed to serve. Hard-nosed hedge funds began to emerge, buying shares with the express purpose of lobbying firms for major changes to their financial and operational strategies.

In the prevailing management thinking, the concept of "shareholder value" took precedence. This was increasingly reflected in executive compensation structures, with a large percentage of managers' pay linked to stock prices, earnings per share and other market-based measures. But in steering companies to maximise share prices and payouts to investors, worries about excessive and single-minded short-termism arose. The CFO was charged with balancing the long-term interests of the company with the short-term whims of the market, all the while on the defensive against a potential hostile takeover. Although finance chiefs exercised considerable influence internally, around this time they were thrust into the public spotlight like never before, acting as a spokesperson to the markets on investor conference calls, at public presentations and in the media.[3]

Too many chiefs

Only around half of large US firms formally appointed a CFO in the late 1980s. The role's rapid rise to ubiquity since then reflects how crucial it has become in boardrooms around the world.

Perhaps the best way to put the rise of the CFO in context is to compare it with other "chiefs" of similar stature. When the conglomerate reigned and companies competed primarily on their manufacturing prowess, chief operating officers (COOs) were more prevalent than chief financial officers. But as firms were forced to refocus, and the burdens of managing investors and analysts grew, chief executive officers (CEOs) saw financial experts as the ideal second-in-command, bestowing on them a new title and privileged status. Responsibility for running day-to-day operations, the domain of the COO, was pushed down to divisional presidents; at headquarters, the monitoring and co-ordination role was divvied up between the CEO and CFO. Once again, GE was an early adopter; it did away with its group-level COO role in 1983.

An academic study of large US firms since the 1960s found that CEO-COO duos dominated until the mid-1980s, when they were overtaken by CEO-CFO teams. Around 35% of companies employ a COO today, according to Crist/Kolder Associates, a recruitment company (see Figure 1.1); nearly all have an identifiable CFO in the executive committee, if not the full board of directors.

The decline of the COO does not imply a loss of operational knowledge in the executive suite. Career paths in the finance department are less narrowly defined than in the recent past; the majority of CFOs at large companies now spend time outside the finance function on their way to the top finance post. A growing number of finance chiefs are also given responsibility for a key business unit or customer segment on top of their financial duties. According to Suzzane Wood, who leads the European financial officers practice at Russell Reynolds, a recruitment company:

FIG 1.1 **Percentage of companies[a] with a chief operating officer**
%

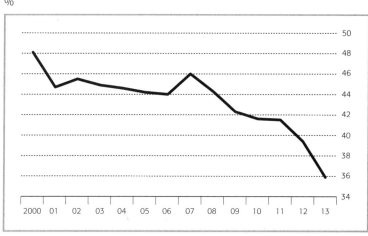

a *Fortune* 500 and S&P 500 (668 companies in 2013).
Source: Crist/Kolder Associates

> *Over the past decade, to be a CFO successor you need experience*
> *in a regional or divisional role, a corporate role and general*
> *management. CFO is a business-leadership role, and those things*
> *make you a business leader rather than a functional leader.*

Called to account

The CFO's influence as an active operator rather than a passive adviser
was demonstrated, rather unfortunately, by a series of scandals in
the early 2000s. The authority of the CFO came to the attention of
the general public when a number of them were caught inflating
revenues, hiding losses and otherwise abusing their authority. Falling
stockmarkets in the wake of the dotcom bust exposed the wrongdoing,
which in most cases was motivated by the need to meet aggressive
targets pledged by the executives to investors.

Among the most notable companies to fall from grace were
Enron, WorldCom and Tyco in the United States, and Ahold and
Parmalat in Europe.[4] Tellingly, government prosecutors relied
heavily on co-operation from CFOs to build their cases against chief
executives and chairmen at these firms. Andrew Fastow of Enron

and Scott Sullivan of WorldCom became household names. No fewer than five former CFOs of HealthSouth pled guilty to fraud as the US government targeted the hospital group's founder and CEO. Invariably, chief executives cited CFOs as the "architects" and "masterminds" of the frauds, pleading ignorance of the day-to-day realities of their companies' operations and financial accounts. A particularly brazen example came from Cees van der Hoeven, CEO of Ahold, a Dutch retailer, who professed a limited knowledge of the company's accounts, despite serving as its CFO before taking over as chief executive. The blame heaped on CFOs also took a personal toll; Fausto Tonna, former CFO of Parmalat, reportedly smashed holes in desks and shattered glass doors. He famously wished reporters "a slow and painful death" outside the prosecutor's office in Parma.

The suggestion that CFOs could orchestrate multibillion-dollar frauds, while certainly unwelcome, underscored the power they commanded at even the largest corporations. The official reaction to these scandals acknowledged as much; the Sarbanes-Oxley Act of 2002 required that CFOs and CEOs at US-listed firms personally certified that a company's financial statements were true, with harsh penalties if inaccuracies later came to light. The act also imposed elaborate requirements on companies to assess and report on the effectiveness of internal control systems. Other countries introduced similar rules, though rarely as harsh as Sarbanes-Oxley, to clarify responsibility for financial reports, bolster internal controls and enhance corporate governance. Although these rules stemmed, in part, from egregious misdeeds on the part of finance chiefs, the net effect was to codify the CFO's role as a partner of the CEO at the top of the corporate pyramid.

Even if the majority of law-abiding CFOs still grumble about Sarbanes-Oxley and its ilk as costly bureaucracy, they did not allow the rules to slow them down for long. In 2007, global mergers and acquisitions (M&A) reached an all-time high, with more than $4 trillion in deals, almost half of which were cross-border transactions. Emerging markets featured in around a quarter of all M&A in 2013, three times the share only ten years earlier.

The global nature of business presents new risks and opportunities for CFOs, in terms of both where their companies operate and how their finance departments are structured. Advances in technology free finance staff from much of the mundane work once required to produce accounts; as a result, CFOs often scatter the brightest finance employees around business units to provide strategic analysis and decision support to divisional directors. The remaining transactional staff can be collected in so-called shared service centres, based in low-cost locations if not outsourced completely.

Opportunity in adversity

The global financial crisis of 2008 thrust CFOs into the spotlight once again. In the West, the severity of the downturn was surpassed only by the Great Depression, when the remit of finance chiefs was much narrower. In recent years, CFOs have scrambled to move cash to safe havens lest it get trapped in a collapsing bank; undoing some of the fiendishly complex derivatives and other financial "innovations" peddled by banks before the crash also took concerted efforts. With credit scarce and expensive, the watchword remains flexibility, with companies cutting costs and conserving – some would say hoarding – cash.

In the beleaguered European telecoms industry, for example, "flat is the new up", according to Timotheus Höttges, CFO of Deutsche Telekom (and CEO from January 2014). Defending the company's existing operations – "strengthening our strengths", as Höttges describes it – takes precedence over growth in new markets, however enticing the prospects. In the current environment, "we cannot allocate our resources all over the place," he says.

At the banks at the centre of the crisis, the influence of the CFO was also prominent. David Viniar, who spent 13 years as finance chief at Goldman Sachs before his retirement in 2013, is credited with a 2006 push to back out of investments in subprime mortgage-linked securities, limiting the damage his bank suffered when the bottom fell out of the market a few years later. Contrast this with Douglas Braunstein, CFO of rival JPMorgan from 2010 to 2013, on whose watch traders saddled the bank with a $6 billion loss. An internal investigation found weak controls partly to blame, chiding Braunstein's finance team for taking "too narrow a view of their responsibilities" in questioning the validity of traders' forecasts that proved dangerously out-of-touch with reality. (The comprehensive failures of risk management at the likes of Lehman Brothers and other bankrupt or bailed-out banks, of course, go without saying.)

Throughout history, in times of crisis companies turn to their CFOs for guidance. Given free rein to steady the corporate ship when times are tough, the authority finance chiefs gain during these episodes never fully recedes once the turmoil is over. Making the transition from cutting costs to promoting growth is never easy, but the history of the CFO position is one of versatility.

In a 1933 report to members of the Controllers Institute, the leadership laid out its plan "to establish the position of the controller in the bylaws of the corporation, rather than by mere appointment and subject to the varying whims of executive officers, as at present so often is the case". In a relatively short time, historically speaking, the role of the CFO has grown from a discretionary clerical post to a vital strategic position whose influence is matched only by the chief executive. But with this new-found power comes a level of responsibility, accountability and visibility that offers as many risks as opportunities.

2 Role: ensuring control, driving strategy

WHAT DOES A CFO DO? For a role with such a clear-cut title, the answer can be complicated. It depends, in part, on a company's size and line of business, as well as its state of health. Whatever the case, most finance chiefs say that they spend, ideally, no more than half of their time on purely financial matters. The balance is generally devoted to acting as a "business partner", an area open to interpretation. At root, it is about bringing the CFO's knowledge and command of a company's financial resources to serve broad strategic goals. Put another way, it is actively plotting a company's future course rather than passively recording where it has been.

"Every element of business decision-making has a financial element to it," notes Tim Haywood, finance chief at Interserve, a UK-listed construction and support services group. "This gives the CFO a unique vista and sphere of influence."

CFOs use this influence in different ways. Finance's access to information from all corners of a firm – everyone must answer to this department at some point – gives CFOs a comprehensive view of company performance. From this perch, finance chiefs must strike a balance between serving as an adviser to managers and leading them in a particular direction.

In a 2012 global survey of senior finance executives by Michael Page International, a recruitment company, two-thirds of respondents described themselves as a supportive "developer" or proactive "leader", with leader the marginally more popular choice. (In North America, nearly 60% of CFOs considered themselves leaders, whereas in Europe there was a roughly equal share of leaders and developers.) In a similar poll in 2013 by Accenture, Oracle and

Longitude Research, although more than 70% of CFOs said that their level of strategic influence had risen in recent years, they ranked their role in the "validation" of strategy as more important than the part they play in the "formulation" of strategic plans. This combination of supporter and leader, of appraiser and creator, explains why the CFO is often described as a co-pilot, shifting between monitor and driver depending on the circumstances.

Role playing

As one of the world's oldest accountancy bodies, the Institute of Chartered Accountants in England and Wales (ICAEW) benefits from a uniquely long historical perspective when it considers the role of the CFO. The institute's research arm has published extensively on the subject, taking advantage of its well-established position in the UK to track the evolution of the top finance post.

In 1963, Stanley Harding, a finance executive at Shell, gave a speech to ICAEW members in Cambridge. As the modern conception of the CFO was only beginning to emerge (see Chapter 1), Harding described the three hats that finance chiefs were required to wear at the time:

- Financial expert – monitor of potential shortfalls in the "component items of profitability" in the short term and weaknesses in "cash generation, liquidity and investment" in the long term.
- Member of the management team – judge of priorities during the planning cycle, making sure forecasts are "genuine targets and not just vague hopes".
- Manager of the financial and accounting staff – motivator of finance staff whose work may lack "the same stimulus or glamour as there is, for instance, in selling products".

Taking a cue from Harding, the ICAEW revisited the CFO's remit nearly 50 years later (Richard Young, "The seven hats of the FD", *Finance and Management*, December 2011). Today, finance chiefs wear seven different hats, according to the institute. This is, presumably, a reflection of the ever-expanding role of the finance chief and not a comment on the size of CFOs' heads:

- Storyteller – creator of a clear narrative for internal and external audiences.

- Co-pilot – partner to the CEO with a complementary skill set.
- Magistrate – arbiter of disputes and enforcer of the law.
- Consigliere – trusted counsel, offering advice at the highest level.
- Engineer – master of processes and systems; architect of business models.
- Muse – promoter of fresh thinking and value-enhancing decisions.
- Rescue service – identifier of problems and presenter of solutions.

Navigation partner

One thing CFOs universally reject is the caricature of "Dr No", the overly cautious administrator obsessed with cutting costs and prone to reject any proposal to spend money. Jeff van der Eems, promoted from CFO of United Biscuits, a food company, to head of its international operations in mid-2013, says:

> I don't like descriptions like "gatekeeper" or "guardian" because it gives the impression that you're stopping business rather than finding reasons to make it work. Good finance people find reasons to say "yes", but make sure that it's done in the right way.

In other words, in validating a colleague's strategic proposal, the CFO may introduce important alterations or suggest alternative courses of action, thereby becoming a partner in the formulation of an initiative. Van der Eems likens this to the role of a navigator:

> Business is a journey. The CFO helps shape the vision – the destination – and makes sure the milestones are clear, monitoring progress along the way and correcting course where necessary. It's a positive partnering role, with a strong control element.

In treading the line between monitor and partner, finance chiefs emphasise the importance of their independence; few business heads argue for smaller budgets or to deprioritise their projects, so it is up to the CFO to weigh projects on their individual merits as well as how they contribute to a coherent corporate whole. This is how Alan Williams, CFO of Greencore, a Dublin-based convenience food company, puts it:

The role of the CFO is to be able to step out of the detail and emotion of the situation and become a dispassionate observer. One of the most underrated CFO skills is being a calm person. The business needs someone who's calm, logical and rational.

In this regard – and to employ another metaphor – if the CEO is cast as *Star Trek*'s Captain Kirk, the CFO is Mister Spock (his common refrain: "That is illogical, captain").

Jeremy Hope, a consultant, described the principal differences between an accountant and fully-fledged business partner in his book *Reinventing the CFO*:

What do business partners do that accountants don't? ... Their approach to investment proposals and other project-based decisions is constructive scepticism rather than outright cynicism ... They are generally seen as independent members of the team with no vested interests in decision outcomes. Whereas marketing people are focused on market share and production people on volume and quality output, finance people are just interested in making the right decision. And if the risks are too great for the potential returns, they will say so.

The impartial analysis of competing projects and diverse scenarios requires a common means of measurement. Fluency in financial figures – the fundamental measures of value – puts the CFO at the centre of this process. For Jens Madrian, CFO of RWE npower, a UK utility company, one of his main roles is to "take the visionary and intangible and turn it into measurable, operational things".

More often than not, the most important measure for the CFO is cash flow; it is the easiest to measure and the hardest to fudge. A company can survive if it makes losses, but quickly falters when it runs out of cash. Some €1.2 trillion ($1.6 trillion) in payments are processed per year by Visa Europe, so its CFO, Philip Symes, understands this well:

Cash is the lifeblood of a company. If we don't have any, we die. I see my role as ensuring that we have sufficient blood flowing to the right places to keep the organisation healthy.

The easiest way to boost a company's cash balance, of course, is to cut costs and stop spending. But this strategy will not succeed for long. For CFOs to act as credible judges of strategic plans and trusted partners of operational executives, they need to understand how a company generates cash. This means they need to leave their offices and uncover the story behind the numbers.

Out and about

Less than ten years before Denise Ramos took over as CEO of industrial conglomerate ITT in 2011, she found herself touring the kitchen at KFC, a fast-food company, making biscuits and fried chicken. Over the course of a long career in finance, Ramos spent three years as CFO of KFC. She says:

> When I took over as CFO, one of the things I needed to do to really figure things out was to work at a restaurant. It gave me a whole different perspective.

This is a bit extreme, perhaps, but indicative of the broader role that many CFOs now play. Although a business unit's financial results provide the best measure, a nuanced appreciation for the drivers of performance before they are translated into profits and losses is vital. Diane Morefield, CFO of Strategic Hotels & Resorts, a Chicago-based luxury hotel company, describes this as "empathy for how the numbers happen". When she visits one of her company's hotels, a review of its accounts is only one of her goals. Around the property, she looks for signs of a good rapport between managers and rank-and-file staff. If they are on a first-name basis and show one another "sincere warmth and respect", she knows from experience that a positive financial performance should follow.

Contact with customers is also important. Seamus Keating spent 13 years at Logica, an Anglo-Dutch IT services group, eight of them as CFO. A few years into his tenure as finance chief, he took responsibility for the company's financial services practice. This customer-facing role gave him a better view of the business, he says:

> You can get very isolated if you only think about the numbers.
> Understanding what clients want first-hand is a way of sharpening

the edges. It puts you in a powerful position when you think about priorities. The more you can join things up, the more effective you are as a CFO.

Tracey Travis, CFO of Estée Lauder, a cosmetics company, agrees, but sounds a note of caution about striking a balance, as she explained in a report published by Ernst & Young, a professional services firm, when she was CFO of retailer Ralph Lauren:

Ensuring business decisions are grounded in sound financial criteria is a key role, and sometimes the CFO can get distracted with other opportunities that are important to the organisation and are, quite honestly, more intellectually stimulating and more fun.

The marriage of financial acumen with operational savvy is a potent one, establishing the CFO as, effectively, deputy CEO. Instead of distracting them from their basic fiduciary duties, research suggests that these powerful CFOs manage their departments more effectively than less empowered peers.

In a forthcoming study of US firms by Jean Bedard and Rani and Udi Hoitash,[1] companies with their CFO on the board of directors are linked with lower probabilities of financial restatements, internal controls weaknesses and signs of accounting manipulation. In economics, the principal–agent problem suggests that when a CFO joins the board of directors (the company's top decision-making body, the principal), the board's power to monitor and discipline the finance chief (the agent) is reduced, raising the probability of lax controls or self-serving earnings management. That the opposite is true in reality implies CFOs use the power of a seat on the board to bolster internal controls and uphold the integrity of a company's financial systems and processes, not undermine them.

Another study by Andreas Engelen and Andreas Venus, published in 2012, ranked the relative power of CFOs in a sample of companies by their pay, tenure, board presence and related measures. Although strong CFOs did not boost company performance across the board, at highly diversified companies and those pursuing defensive strategies in mature markets, a statistically significant relationship was found between profitability and a CFO's power.

Knowledge is power

The authority of the CFO is evident in other situations, like the trading of company shares. Research[2] shows that CFOs consistently earn better returns than CEOs, COOs and other executives when trading their companies' shares. The effect holds even for CEOs who are former CFOs. One interpretation is that CFOs, by virtue of their position in the top finance post, are more in tune with the prospects for their companies than any of their boardroom colleagues. The more cynical view is that as the executive responsible for compiling and reporting financial results, the CFO is able to massage reported earnings to benefit previous trades.[3]

Less ambiguous evidence of the CFO's influence can be found at family-owned firms. Given the specialised knowledge that the CFO role requires, in many cases the post is the only top management position held by a non-family member. This makes for an ideal natural experiment.

An analysis of German family-owned companies by Ann-Kristin Achleitner, Eva Lutz and Stephanie Schraml found that firms with non-family CFOs were more likely to maintain formal strategic plans – crucial to ensuring the long-term viability of a firm over multiple generations – and make use of multiple bank relationships, suggesting a more sophisticated approach to financing. In Italy, meanwhile, Stephano Caselli and Alberta Di Guili found that non-family CFOs had a significant impact on the profitability of family-owned companies. In fact, the effect grew stronger as successive generations assumed control; as the authors put it, bluntly, professional non-family CFOs "enhance performance and mitigate the ineptness of heirs".

In another domain often criticised for managerial ineptness – government administration – a private-sector-style CFO is often hailed as the solution to myriad problems. Part of the UK Conservative Party's platform ahead of the 2010 general election was to reclassify the finance director as the second highest ranked civil servant in a government department. George Osborne, the Conservative chancellor-to-be, lamented that government finance chiefs were "undervalued and underinvolved", with six central departments spending the equivalent of $70 billion per year without a finance director at the board level. When the state of Michigan took on greater financial oversight for the ailing city of Detroit in 2012, part of the rescue plan included the creation of a CFO post, a first for the city.

Back to basics

The mere presence of a CFO is not enough to guarantee financial success, however broad the role or powerful the individual who holds the position. (Detroit went bankrupt in July 2013.) Following a review of surveys on the role of the corporate finance department, the ICAEW concluded that the language used to describe the CFO's wide-ranging role was somewhat overdone:

> It is possible to get the impression that superhuman CFOs, with highly talented teams, using integrated systems and sophisticated analytical techniques are the main determinant of organisational success. While we do believe that effective finance functions can be an important part of such success it is important that we are more realistic in our expectations.

Indeed, one way to interpret the persistent talk about CFOs' role as business partners is that it reflects aspiration more than reality. Few finance chiefs, after all, argue that they should spend more time on technical accounting matters or transactional issues. Their boardroom colleagues think along similar lines; in a 2013 survey of non-financial executives by Korn/Ferry International, a recruitment company, and CFO magazine, respondents cited "strategic vision" twice as often as any other area when asked what CFOs could improve to add the most value to their companies.

Whatever their background and however their role is structured, good CFOs appreciate that their influence stems from effective stewardship of the finance function. Julian Metherell, CFO of Genel Energy, a UK-listed oil exploration company, says:

> A CFO would be foolish to spend too much time gazing into the strategic future when he's not in control of the day-to-day running of the business.

Jeffrey Thomson, head of the New Jersey-based Institute of Management Accountants, adds:

As mundane as it is, if you don't do the basics well you lose the right to be at the table for higher order types of strategising and envisioning.

The penalties for financial missteps, unsurprisingly, are more severe for CFOs than for any other member of the executive team. In fact, for all the extra responsibilities piled onto finance chiefs, the scope for error in basic financial processes is smaller than ever. A 2009 study by Denton Collins, Adi Masli, Austin Reitenga and Juan Manuel Sanchez of US-listed companies forced to restate earnings reports found that their former CFOs rarely moved to a position with similar seniority at a different company, nor were they as welcome at other listed firms. Following the introduction of the Sarbanes-Oxley Act in 2002, this loss of status became even more pronounced. Keith Williams, CFO-turned-CEO at British Airways, says:

Of all the organisations within a company, finance is expected as much, if not more than most, to do things right. There's a precision there.

Jan Siegmund feels the unique weight of responsibility for control and compliance as CFO of ADP, a staffing and payroll processing group. A former McKinsey management consultant, Siegmund spent 13 years at ADP in a variety of strategy, business development and general management roles. When he was appointed CFO in late 2012, it was his first formal finance role at the firm. Still, as soon as he set foot in his new office, he turned more conservative. "It comes with the job," he says. The scrutiny from investors and regulators, in particular, changed his way of thinking:

Many of the ideas you have as a strategist don't pass the reality check – you can't recognise revenues that way, or you cannot account for something in a certain way. Those are nuisances for a strategist but very important realities for a CFO. I had a lot to learn about that.

This is not to say that Siegmund has lost his strategic drive. His appointment reflects a desire at ADP to "accelerate our innovativeness and aggressiveness in the marketplace," he says. This remains his goal, informed by the fiduciary duties he must fulfil as CFO.

Under pressure

The dark side of the pressure placed on CFOs was highlighted, tragically, by the suicide of Pierre Wauthier, CFO of Zurich Insurance Group, in August 2013. In a note, he reportedly blamed stress stemming from his working relationship with Josef Ackermann, the chairman of the group. Ackermann denied the allegation, and a company investigation later concluded that no "undue or inappropriate pressure" was placed on the CFO. "We are unable to explain the motivation behind his tragic decision," the company said in a statement. Ackermann resigned his position shortly after the suicide.

The interactions between Wauthier and Ackermann were described as "tough but professional" in news reports. Ackermann himself said his relationship with the finance chief was "always businesslike and based on mutual respect". The details of friction between the two revolved around Ackermann's brusque demeanour in board meetings and, specifically, an encounter in which the chairman urged the CFO to express to investors that the company was falling behind in achieving certain long-term financial targets. The CFO reportedly wanted to paint the company's progress in a more positive light. The subsequent earnings presentation, two weeks before Wauthier's suicide, saw the company's share price fall after it acknowledged some of the challenges it faced in meeting the goals it set for itself – the result, it would seem, of a compromise between the chairman's and CFO's positions.

Overall, reports of clashes between the executives suggest a persistent underlying tension and difference of opinion. But many of the accounts of the disagreements would be readily recognisable to finance chiefs at other high-profile companies. It is dangerous to read too much into such a personal and profound tragedy, but it warrants reflection that Wauthier – an outwardly healthy, hard-working family man – cited the stresses of his position as motivation for his fateful decision. Even if not "undue or inappropriate", the personal stress experienced by CFOs can be extreme.

Setting an example

CFOs can make the most of their functional responsibility by promoting finance as a role model for other functions – marketing, IT, human resources and the like – as well as the company as a whole. Jesper Brandgaard, for example, considers one of his main roles as CFO of Novo Nordisk, a Danish pharmaceutical company, is to be its resident "benchmarker". For all measurable activities within the finance department – the time it takes to prepare monthly management accounts or the cost to process an invoice, for example – the CFO assesses his team's performance against data from competitors:

> We will never be able to measure in an absolute sense whether we are the best in finance overall, but there are a lot of areas where we can assess whether we are at least in the top three. The important thing is the ambition – the journey more than the destination.

When he became CFO in 2000, Brandgaard set ambitious new targets for Novo Nordisk's finance team. At the time, the company compared itself with other Nordic companies. The new CFO instead wanted the finance department to use the global pharmaceutical industry as a benchmark – a much tougher standard – and aim to be the best (or at least placed in the top quartile). The use of a relative target ensures continuous efforts to improve, given that competitors will be doing the same.

In achieving its goal to rank at or near the top of global pharmaceutical companies in terms of finance efficiency, Brandgaard's team became the first at the company to set up an offshore shared service centre, in Bangalore. At first, the office handled basic transactional processes like accounts payable. Soon, however, the centre proved adept at taking on higher-value-added tasks at a much lower cost than in Europe or North America. Other parts of the company noticed, and today the office in Bangalore employs workers in finance, human resources, IT, legal and other functions.

Brandgaard's finance team also pioneered the creation of a global functional board, which brings finance managers from key units around the world together to meet every quarter. Under the company's decentralised structure, regional finance directors report to the local general manager instead of the CFO at corporate headquarters. The finance board creates a sense of community among the far-flung finance team, and also provides a venue to share experiences and co-ordinate global finance initiatives (like the Bangalore shared service centre). There are now a host of similar functional boards for Novo Nordisk's other functions, following finance's lead.

Despite their lofty positions, CFOs lack the ultimate authority of the CEO, so their influence outside the finance function must rely on the power of persuasion. Thus, when finance chiefs urge others to improve efficiency or effectiveness, the message carries more sway if their own department can demonstrate the benefits – if, in other words, they eat their own cooking. (This is particularly useful if the dish appears unpalatable at first, as with any cost-cutting exercise.)

In many ways, the finance department serves as the ideal proving ground: it features multi-level hierarchies; a diverse range of jobs, from the most basic to the extremely complex; and a wide variety of activities, from inward-facing support services like accounting to externally focused activities like investor relations. To paraphrase Frank Sinatra, if the CFO proves that a plan can make it there, it will make it anywhere.

Italian drama

A CFO's influence tends to fluctuate according to the health of a company. That is, CFOs gain the most power when their companies are in the worst shape.

Monte dei Paschi di Siena, Italy's third-largest bank, was founded in 1472 and is by most accounts the oldest bank in the world. When it plunged into crisis in 2012, it installed a new management team, including Bernardo Mingrone as CFO. Only 38 when appointed, Mingrone is one of the youngest finance chiefs of a large listed company in Europe.

The first-time CFO was not daunted by the bank's long history – and even if he had been, there was no time to dwell on it. The new executive team uncovered evidence of hidden losses and shadowy derivatives deals shortly after it took over; the contract detailing several ill-judged transactions was squirreled away in a safe that the new management discovered almost a year after they took over. As well as generating criminal investigations of former managers, these transactions saddled the bank with unwelcome write-downs at an already difficult time; the bank recorded a collective loss of nearly €8 billion in 2011 and 2012. A €4 billion state bail-out was agreed in early 2013. To avoid full nationalisation, the bank aims to reduce operating costs by €440m, or 40%, by 2017.

Mingrone, a globe-trotting former investment banker, found the slow pace of the work at the august institution jarring at first. Since "crash therapy" was needed, he says some of his earliest actions addressed his immediate team. Replacements were needed in accounting and control, given the now apparent shortcomings in these areas, as well as other finance posts once held by managers now under suspicion for fraud. But other finance employees rejected the pace of change imposed by the new CFO; on at least one occasion a departing manager slammed the door in his face on the way out. Mingrone says:

> It is better to recruit someone who is young, smart and hungry than someone with experience but not as committed. Today, we need a lot of physical energy and vigour.

To support his many urgent projects, he also created a special unit to deal with the sale of assets, unwinding of minority shareholdings, preparing material for board meetings and other pressing tasks – the equivalent of a financial special forces team.

Monte dei Paschi plans to cut 8,000 jobs, around a quarter of its staff, by 2017 (no mean feat given Italy's powerful unions). Many of the cuts fall on the finance department, including more than 2,300 back-office positions due to be outsourced. Sympathetic to the human toll of layoffs and the effect on employee morale, the bank worked out a creative deal with the unions in which an early-retirement scheme is funded by remaining employees forgoing pay for six days a year for three years. This demonstrated a key strength of the bank's deep heritage – such loyalty and personal sacrifice marked a departure from the culture of Wall Street investment banks where Mingrone got his start.

The sensitivities around personnel decisions fade when the CFO turns to other sources of savings, namely overblown expenses and unnecessary overheads. In these areas, "cutting costs is fun", he says:

> We are trying to become a paperless bank. How do you enforce it? You get rid of printers – there is only one per floor. We have turned down the

heating a couple of notches. The offices were being cleaned five times a week, three times a day – we scaled that down. We turned off company mobiles over the weekend. We cut the fuel allowance for cars and everyone travels second-class. These are drops in the ocean, but people notice.

Even bigger savings were generated when the CFO got tough with suppliers. The idea that you never let a crisis go to waste, typically espoused by hard-nosed politicians, applies in this case. Given the bank's perilous state, simply asking for discounts from IT providers yielded immediate savings. The well-publicised plan to close 550 branches also gave the CFO leverage over the bank's landlords; if they didn't want one of their properties to close, they were urged to cut the rent. By mid-2013, more than 600 rental agreements had been renegotiated.

The cost cuts led by the CFO will account for a majority of the bank's operating profits up to 2017. But whatever the eventual outcome for Monte dei Paschi, Mingrone sees value in the experience, however harrowing:

My role as CFO today is like a fireman putting out fires. It is unpleasant at times, particularly the human aspect of things. But the truth is, this is exciting.

In any cost-cutting exercise, diminishing returns eventually set in. Given his age and experience, Mingrone is on track for a CEO-type role in the future, which he confirms is a career goal. Few CFOs cut their way to the top, however appropriate aggressive action is during the depths of crisis.

Mingrone is acutely aware of the need to be tough without alienating himself from colleagues; in his office hangs a framed document issued in 1629 by the bank's board of directors, which at that time wielded extensive powers in Tuscany. In response to alleged misdeeds by Armenio Melari, the bank's *camerlengo* (finance chief), the board's edict sentenced him to death by hanging.

People power

Somewhat paradoxically, the rise of the CFO in terms of profile is mirrored by a steady shrinkage of the finance department in terms of budget. The finance chief's power does not derive from a large, lavishly equipped financial army – quite the opposite.

FIG 2.1 **Finance cost as percentage of revenue: global 1,000 companies**

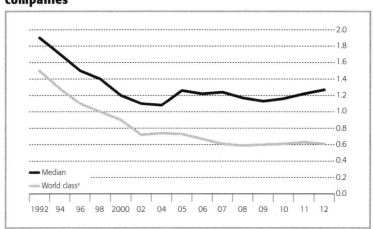

a Median of companies in top quartile of both cost and effectiveness.
Source: The Hackett Group

In 2012, operating costs for the finance department at a typical large company were 1.3% of revenues, according to The Hackett Group, a consultancy (see Figure 2.1). Although somewhat higher than in recent years, this was some 30% less than 20 years ago, despite the exponential growth in the volume and sophistication of demands placed on the department over this period.

When Hackett surveyed finance executives in early 2013, their expectation for revenues and finance budgets implied an average "productivity gap" of 10% – that is, the difference between the rate of growth in revenues and the decrease in the finance department's budget. But this need not imply a drop in effectiveness; Hackett's benchmark addresses the balance between efficiency and efficacy. (Simply running a tight ship is not enough, as the quality of services can suffer; superior services, meanwhile, may prove ruinously expensive.) Companies that scored in the top quartile of both efficiency and effectiveness spent only 0.6% of revenues on finance in 2012, some 60% less than top performers 20 years ago.[4] This means that for every $1 billion in sales, world-class finance departments save nearly $7m in costs compared with the industry median. These top-ranked finance departments are also able to devote 60% of their time to value-added analysis and 40% to basic data collection; at the median company, this proportion is reversed.

Automation and outsourcing explain much of the drop in finance costs since the 1990s. The levelling-off in recent years suggests that further improvements are harder to achieve. But the gap between average and top performers is wider than ever, with the best companies keeping costs steady while they creep up elsewhere. With the finance department's work expected only to increase, one of the CFO's biggest challenges is to convince team members to do more with less. Attracting, retaining and motivating the right people is therefore of paramount importance.

The qualities that companies look for in a CFO today are leadership, communication skills and finance savvy, according to Wolfgang Schmidt-Soelch, a partner at Korn/Ferry in Zurich and former CFO of Winterthur, an insurance company. These are in order of importance, he notes, as finance knowledge is such a given these days that "you almost don't need to put it on the list". Anyway, a CFO's ability to organise and lead the finance function is the true key to success; gaps in a CFO's financial expertise can be filled by recruiting team members with complementary skills.

Brandgaard of Novo Nordisk says that people-related issues have been his "most profound focus" in recent years. When the finance function achieved the initial efficiency targets set out in its benchmarking exercise, a new plan was hatched to "put business partnering at the centre of what we do," he says. The goal, according to the CFO, is for the finance department to become "a net exporter of talent" to other functions and departments at Novo Nordisk. The ultimate business partner, after all, is someone who is equally fluent in finance and operations.

This migration of talent from finance to other parts of the business helps boost the financial savvy of all employees, easing the burden on the finance department and reducing the distractions and stress that can lead to misjudgments and errors. This is clear to Peter Kellogg, CFO of Merck, a US pharmaceutical company, in the context of the $8 billion that the company spends on developing new medicines each year, as he explained to CFO magazine:

Because so much is being invested and there is so much uncertainty, having the entire organisation develop a certain level of financial literacy in terms of how you sequence your work, how much of a risk you take, is there a good return on investment, what are the trade-offs you have to make as you're developing or commercialising drugs – that's tremendously valuable.

Zarin Patel, CFO at the BBC from 2004 to 2013, likes to call herself a "chief performance officer" instead of chief financial officer. The narrower remit implied by the traditional title ignores that the CFO's domain has transformed "from a classic finance function to a comprehensive business function," she says.

Performance, in a business context, entails a balance between cost and value. This is similar to the CFO's role as a strict enforcer of financial controls as well as a freethinking, forward-looking strategist. To this end, a sharp mind and clarity of purpose are important qualities for any CFO. But because the role is far too big for anyone to take on alone, finance chiefs who carefully build and motivate teams to support them are the ones who thrive instead of merely survive. This is a common theme in the next chapter, about the CFO's core areas of responsibility.

3 Responsibilities: internal affairs

IN THE FINANCE DEPARTMENT, there is a natural rhythm that comes from the monthly, quarterly and annual reporting cycles, and other routine activities from accounting consolidation to tax reporting and payroll processing. At the CFO level, however, there is little contact with these basic processes, even in smaller companies with limited finance support. Bobby Foley, finance chief at 192.com, an online directory company, says:

> Some people think I just sit in a room and play with numbers all day. But I haven't done the monthly management accounts in years.

There is little routine in the day-to-day duties of a CFO.

A goal for most finance chiefs is to centralise the functions that perform standardised, high-volume processes, and appoint specialists to streamline these routine transactional processes. Once established, these units are often sited in low-cost locations or outsourced to third-party service providers.[1] What remains is not easily compartmentalised, like investment analysis and risk management, or is less predictable, like capital raising and M&A. Across all these areas, the CFO plays a crucial role in establishing priorities and setting strategy. This makes for a varied schedule, as Jean-Marc Duplaix, CFO of Kering (formerly known as PPR), a French luxury goods company, explained to CFO.com:

> When I'm at our headquarters in Paris, I try to spend 12 hours a day at the office. We have all these projects to manage, and I have several meetings in a day on topics like information-system projects and real estate issues – for example, opening of new stores. We have

*discussions around profitability expected from the stores. I also
need two or three hours to be quiet and to think about long-term
issues. The rest of the time I have meetings with teams, advisers and
management.*

Closer to a quarter- or year-end reporting date, a CFO's schedule
will feature chunkier accounting, reporting and regulatory issues.
Acquisitions and disposals muscle in on a finance chief's diary
during the dealmaking process, regardless of other commitments. The
typically spartan office of a large-company CFO also reflects plenty
of time spent on the road, meeting far-flung colleagues, investors,
bankers and service providers. If anything, 12 hours in the office
discussing projects and performance – with a few hours spare to
consider long-term strategy – is a rather tranquil day.

No CFO's remit is the same as another's. Listed companies face
more regulatory responsibilities than private firms. A family-owned
business may put different pressures on a CFO than a private equity-
owned company would. Group-level finance chiefs are responsible
for activities that divisional CFOs are not. Reporting lines in finance
departments vary widely, even among otherwise identical firms.

This chapter addresses the CFO's core responsibilities – it is not a
complete catalogue of the finance department's various duties. The
decisions a finance chief makes in these key areas, while often high-
level in nature, have important implications that are felt across the
company. They range from the short-term and transactional to the
long-term and strategic (and are discussed in roughly this order).

Accounting, controlling and reporting

The finance department's fundamental duty, to compile a company's
accounts, can be unusually fraught. Bruce Nolop, former CFO of
E*Trade, a US-based financial services company, and Pitney Bowes, a
business services provider, describes the potential sources of tension
in his book *The Essential CFO*:

*Given the regularity of the reporting schedule, companies may have
a tendency to take their processes for granted. However, they can be
quite complex, usually involving numerous judgments, substantial*

data manipulation, and intensive co-ordination among a number of people in disparate roles and possibly remote locations.

Although accounting matters are typically delegated to the senior controller, if something goes wrong it is the CFO who gets it in the neck. In the United States, external auditors are required to test and report on the strength of a company's internal controls – they must issue a dreaded "material weakness" notice if they find a serious deficiency in, say, the way revenue is recorded for products not yet shipped or the time it takes to reconcile intercompany transactions in the general ledger.

If a breakdown in controls also leads to a restatement of previously published financial results, quite often it costs CFOs their job. A controls weakness alone leads to a 15% cut in the CFO's average bonus payment, a 2012 study by Rani and Udi Hoitash and Karla Johnstone found. Although CEOs share the same legal responsibility in attesting to the accuracy of a company's accounts, their compensation is unaffected. Indeed, companies with CEOs and directors with former finance experience punish their CFOs more severely when controls break down, cutting pay more deeply than average.

All CFOs say that their companies' accounting policies and controls are conservative, but in reality wide discretion is allowed. The costs of elaborate controls – like a strict segregation of duties or multiple sign-offs for certain expenditures – are more apparent than the benefits. Like a referee in sport, successful controls enforce the rules without being noticed; if they noisily assert themselves at every turn, complaints about gratuitous obstruction arise. Even after controlling for relative levels of spending on research and development, studies have found that a company's degree of accounting conservatism is inversely related to its portfolio of patents, one measure of innovation.[2]

How much leeway do CFOs have when it comes to accounting results? More than you might think. In a survey by Ilia Dichev, John Graham, Campbell Harvey and Shive Rajgopal, a group of finance chiefs at listed companies, said 50% of reported earnings is driven by innate factors beyond managerial control. The other half can be massaged, so to speak; the poll suggests a fifth of firms flatter their result in some way, on average by 10% of earnings per share.

For a profession with a black-and-white image, these are considerable shades of grey. The temptation to break the rules, instead of merely bend them, is great. Just ask Andrew Fastow. After serving more than five years in prison for his part in accounting fraud at Enron, Fastow explained his role in the deceit at a June 2013 conference for fraud examiners:

> I knew that what I was doing was misleading. But I didn't think it was illegal. I thought: That's how the game is played. You have a complex set of rules, and the objective is to use the rules to your advantage. And that was the mistake I made.

There are plenty of ways to interpret accounting rules that will not land a CFO in jail. One of the most popular earnings "games" CFOs play is the year-end shuffling of working capital – bringing sales forward and pushing payments out in an attempt to boost the all-important fourth-quarter results. REL, a consultancy, reports that nearly half of the 1,000 largest listed non-financial firms in the United States engage in this practice. At these companies, net working capital – roughly, inventory and accounts receivable less accounts payable – fell by \$52 billion from the third to the fourth quarter in 2011, then bounced back by \$53 billion in the first quarter of 2012. (The lower the working capital, the better.) In a report, REL bemoans the practice:

> Ironically, the amount of time, effort and money that companies invest in this practice every quarter- and year-end far surpasses the effort to establish processes and procedures that, when run efficiently, help create conditions for working capital performance that would minimise and probably eliminate the need to play these games.

Still, the games go on. It is not surprising that there is evidence that this might be linked to bonus payments. Compared with other executives, including the CEO, the size of bonuses awarded to CFOs is more strongly linked to a variety of signs of "earnings management", to employ a common euphemism. If boards want "to weaken incentive pay to get more truthful reporting, diluting the CFO's bonus and stock options would be one place to start," according to research by

Felix Oberholzer-Gee and Julie Wulf, professors at Harvard Business School.[3] Most CFOs resent the suggestion that they act in such naked self-interest. Indeed, finance chiefs' accounting policy preferences have been shown to endure as they move from one company to another, despite different pay policies.

In a typical year, US-listed companies make more than 1,000 restatements and adjustments to published financials, three-quarters of which are minor, according to Audit Analytics, a research firm. This imprecision, companies argue, stems from the combination of increasingly complex global operations, stricter regulations and the proliferation of ambiguous new accounting rules. The sheer volume of information that companies are required to produce is an indication of this growing burden; the length of the average UK-listed company's annual report ran to 103 pages in 2012, double the size in 2000. Firms with securities registered in the United States published reports twice as long as the average; HSBC's blockbuster 2012 annual report was nearly 550 pages.

Thus the reporting process can be anything but routine. CFOs exert considerable influence over accounting interpretations and the strictness of controls, key components in the risk-reward equation for financial reporting. These choices are reflected in the time it takes from the end of an accounting period to the announcement of audited results – the speed of the so-called "close cycle" is a symptom of the overall health of a company's accounting processes, according to BPM International, a consultancy:

> It represents the health of the financial information supply chain across the entire organisation, from the effectiveness of transaction processing systems across the globe, through the state of the general ledger systems, to the effectiveness and discipline around accounting policies, finance education, training and partnering in the organisation.

Accounting and controlling staff generally form one of the largest groups in the finance department. A CFO's policy decisions are clearly influential when it comes to the proficiency of a company's accounting processes, but old-fashioned leadership is equally important. Erich

Hunziker, former CFO of Roche, a Swiss pharmaceutical company, explained how he pushed his team to cut the time it took to close the books to *HQ Asia* magazine:

> We did this through the brutal openness of peer pressure, where anyone could go into the system and see which legal entity in the group had missed its reporting deadline and why. Some managers balked at this initially, especially if it was due to computer issues that their legal entity ended up looking poorly to the rest of the group. My response was, "Sorry, next month you can show you have everything under control." More importantly, it is not a culture of excuse we want to build, but a culture of fact. In addition, it is a fact that the group cannot close on time if one legal entity cannot deliver on time.

Although speed is not the only goal in financial reporting, it is usually how non-financial colleagues judge the competence of the finance department. Despite the pressure this puts on finance chiefs, every CFO must strike a balance between speed, accuracy and cost. (This is generally subject to the ironclad law of the service industry: "fast, good, cheap: pick any two".) Accounting and controlling may seem mundane to others but, given the penalties for getting it wrong, it is an area no finance chief can afford to neglect.

Taxing times

As the CFO of Starbucks, an international coffee purveyor with $13 billion in annual revenues, Troy Alstead is used to speaking to large audiences, be it employees, investors or the media. In late 2012, he faced one of his toughest crowds yet.

Hauled before a UK parliamentary committee, Alstead answered thorny questions about how much tax Starbucks paid in the UK. At issue was the seemingly small amount of tax paid by the company, despite its ubiquitous outlets and apparently healthy trade. Along with representatives from Amazon and Google, who appeared at the hearing for the same reasons, Alstead explained to annoyed MPs why the chain's meagre profits in the country warranted its small (or non-existent) tax bill.

FIG 3.1 **Corporate profits and taxes in the United States**
Quarterly data, seasonally adjusted annual rate, $ billion

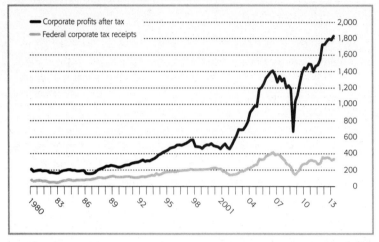

Source: US Federal Reserve

CFOs normally only delve into tax issues with specialists on their teams or analysts tweaking their models on conference calls. This unusually public airing of tax arrangements – which subsequently drew scrutiny for Apple, Facebook, Vodafone and others in Europe and the United States – suggests that it is no longer so obscure.

Of course, when confronted with allegations like the ones facing Starbucks, most companies resort to bland statements like "we pay all applicable taxes in every jurisdiction in which we operate". This is true, but the clever strategies that legally minimise tax are now so effective (see Figure 3.1) that they attract opprobrium in the court of public opinion. For CFOs, what is good for investors and owners (higher profits due to lower taxes) may land their companies in trouble with regulators and customers, who claim that companies are not paying their fair share.

The use of transfer pricing – charges that one corporate entity levies on another in the same group – to concentrate profits in low-tax jurisdictions is a well-established practice. Starbucks in the UK pays subsidiaries in Switzerland and the Netherlands for ingredients and intellectual property, limiting its profits. Political leaders have been making noises about curtailing some aspects of this practice through international forums such as the G20 and OECD.

Co-ordination on such a sensitive sovereign subject is unlikely in the short term, but reconciling a company's complex tax arrangements with its basic operational realities – selling a cup of coffee, say – will present new challenges to CFOs. Facing the threat of boycotts and other bad press, Starbucks pledged to pay the equivalent of $32m more in UK corporate tax in 2013–14 than it otherwise owed.

Planning and analysis

Jack Welch, former head of GE, was no fan of the annual budgeting process. "It sucks the energy, time, fun and big dreams out of an organisation," he wrote in his book *Winning*. Companies succeed in spite of their budgets, not because of them, he claims.

And yet GE continues to produce something that closely resembles a budget. Each of its businesses produces what is known as a "Growth Playbook", as a 2012 report from the group's financial services arm, GE Capital, explains:

> We consider how we have performed against the previous year's goals, and look at both the present and future of our market. In light of those market conditions, we analyse our strengths, weaknesses and future prospects. Then, we set the strategy for meeting our growth targets and we consider the key actions necessary to implement the strategy, including how we will manage potential downsides and how we will keep our strategy on track. Finally, we consider the three-year financial implications and measures of our plan.

Strictly speaking, planning is a more strategic, long-term process than budgeting. The targets and forecasts that inform a plan, however, are inevitably expressed – in some form or another – in monthly, quarterly or annual budgets. It is down to the CFO to decide whether this serves as a useful guide to measure progress towards goals or, as Welch suggests, a wasted effort on something that is outdated and ignored as soon as it is published.

The accounting, controlling and reporting processes built to satisfy regulatory requirements are not well-suited for timely, forward-looking information on company performance. Thus the CFO's financial planning and analysis team (usually shortened to FP&A) is charged with maintaining plans, forecasts and – yes – budgets to monitor and motivate the rest of the business, often working in the divisions alongside business-unit managers. Most CFOs say that this is the area where it is hardest to hire qualified staff, given the commercial savvy required.

It is an area that has grown in importance and sophistication in recent history, as Kuah Boon Wee, CFO-turned-CEO at MTQ, a Singapore-based engineering group, explained in a report published by KPMG, a professional services firm:

> I think when we all started doing accounting, there was something miraculous about a skill in terms of being able to balance the books. You know, prepare the general ledgers and all that. Essentially, all that is now driven by systems. You are no longer in an era where there is something magical about manipulating the data; the data is a function of what goes in, and it's really about interpretation.

One of the biggest mistakes in budgeting is to treat it like a statutory accounting exercise; producing a budget is not a goal in itself, but rather a means to an end. Some companies do away with the traditional annual budget entirely, arguing that it imposes artificial deadlines on firms and promotes counterproductive behaviour among managers keen to hit their targets by any means necessary. These companies typically maintain some form of rolling quarterly forecast, making managers responsible for updating plans continuously instead of during a one-off annual scramble. (This approach is particularly popular in Scandinavia and many proponents of the bin-the-budget school belong to a group called the Beyond Budgeting Roundtable.)

However a company decides to do it, the FP&A function plays a crucial role in collecting and sharing information with business units. When CFOs talk about their partnering role, this is usually the team they have in mind. The challenge is to ensure that relevant, actionable information flows from this team, according to Jeff van der Eems at United Biscuits:

I still get a lot of business data, but not as much business intelligence as I would like. I crave people who can understand the data well enough to say, "Here's the story". I get more people saying, "Let me show you another page of numbers and variances". I don't want that. I want to know what is happening, what are the implications, what are our choices and what do you recommend?

At United Biscuits, the shift from merely sifting through data to generating valuable insights is helped, in part, by outsourcing back-office accounting functions. This allows finance staff to focus on interpreting data instead of collecting it. "You don't produce a report," Van der Eems says. "You get a report and your job is to tell us what it means."

CFOs often describe this information in terms of scorecards and dashboards. Determining what is shared with managers via these tools is a careful exercise in curation. Bombarding managers with too many measures leads to confusion and paralysis; sharing too few measures renders the exercise meaningless. A trial-and-error approach is sometimes employed; if the finance department unilaterally stops producing a report and managers don't complain (or even seem to notice), it was probably not worth producing in the first place.

Robert Simons, a professor at Harvard Business School, reckons that managers should be held accountable for seven measures (plus or minus two), because that is the limit of what most people can easily recall. For CFOs and their analysis-focused teams, meticulous judgment is required to determine which indicators are most important among the mass of information at their disposal. Some, or even most, of these measures will be non-financial.

There is a good reason for this. "If a business operates on purely financial targets, the easiest way to meet those targets is to stop investing," says Jackie Hunt, former CFO of Norwich Union and Standard Life, both insurance companies, and now chief executive at Prudential UK & Europe, another insurance company. When she was finance chief at Standard Life, the company's "balanced scorecard" was evenly split between financial, capital, employee and strategy-related indicators.

Jan Siegmund of ADP describes one of his jobs as "expanding the toolset" that his finance team tracks on behalf of the company. The CFO is using his consulting and strategy background to change the way that ADP assesses the performance of its divisions:

> We are shifting from a classic profit-and-loss-oriented view to a more shareholder-return-oriented assessment of business performance. That is something that is clear to someone who has done a lot of M&A and built business cases with net present values, but for the finance function it is a bit of a shift. Business units that were once kings of the world because of high margins and big profits look very different in a total shareholder return environment, where the rate of change and total lifetime profitability play a bigger role.

By introducing a longer-term, market-oriented view of performance, Siegmund is one of many CFOs trying to promote a better understanding of the link between operational activities and financial outcomes. This pushes finance departments to collect, analyse and share a wider range of information. Karen Hoguet, CFO of Macy's, a US retailer, told the *Wall Street Journal*:

> One of the problems today is that we rely on all these computer reports – we know what customers buy, and how rapid the sell-through is on any given item – but no report will tell you how much they would have bought if things had been different.

At ADP, Siegmund is addressing this challenge by incorporating marketing-derived measures like win-loss ratios against competitors, client satisfaction and net promoter scores alongside traditional financial measures in the company's dashboards.

In a variation of an oft-cited quotation, Niels Bohr, a Danish physicist, said: "Prediction is very difficult, especially about the future." By using its access to information and understanding of the principal business drivers, the finance function plays a crucial role in helping managers make smarter decisions, whatever the situation. The budget may be a blunt tool in this regard, but it reflects – ideally – extensive co-operation between finance and the rest of the business, hatching the forecasts and plans that will guide a company to financial success.

Investment analysis

Before a forecast becomes a plan, or a plan becomes a budget, CFOs help set the overall strategy for the sources and uses of capital. Finance chiefs establish priorities and the sequencing of initiatives, vetting business cases on their individual merits as well as how well they fit with the company's chosen direction.

The returns on capital investments are judged against alternative uses of a company's resources, from acquisitions to dividends, share buy-backs or simply keeping cash in reserve against unforeseen events. The cost of raising funds – be it via internal cash generation or external financing – is a key consideration, as it sets the bar against which all potential returns are measured. That said, a mechanical approach to approving projects based solely on whether they cover their cost of capital is short-sighted; a high-return project may depress short-term earnings at an inopportune time, while crucial investments in risk prevention may offer low or unquantifiable returns on paper. The ordering of projects can also affect potential returns, prompting CFOs to use their central perch to identify dependencies and co-ordinate projects across a company's portfolio accordingly.

When managers compete for resources, if business plans don't pass muster with the CFO, they are unlikely to see the light of day. This is no easy task. "I was born sceptical, which is probably a good quality for a finance director," says Peter Harris, a veteran finance chief at several media and marketing companies in London, most recently Next Fifteen, a communications group. "You don't take anything at face value."

Philip Bowcock, CFO of Cineworld, a UK cinema chain, is also no pushover:

> I like playing the role of devil's advocate. And this isn't always on the negative side. The role of the CFO is to propose a balanced view, to pose the opposite opinion to someone and make them think outside the box occasionally. I can totally agree with what somebody is saying, but I will still go out of my way to point out the opposite view.

These challenges sharpen business plans, Bowcock says. But there is a fine line between being justifiably tough and counterproductively hostile. Nesta, a UK non-profit company that promotes innovation, described this tension in a report about CFOs' relationship with "blue sky" investment proposals:

> Finance executives, by nature and training, can be the most risk-averse decision-makers in the boardroom. They are in their comfort zones when they demand hard numbers and rock-solid business cases before giving new ideas a green light for funding – and with their own knowledge that getting a grip on the intangible benefits of innovation can defy their classic financial training – this often puts them at odds with other parts of the company.

David Bloom is co-founder of fdu group, a London-based agency that places interim CFOs at growing companies. During his many stints as finance chief at a variety of firms, he says the outright rejection of a proposal is rare. Instead, ideas that need work are pushed to the end of the queue until their advocates refine their pitches and bring them back to the CFO. A finance chief's judgment of priorities may also delay otherwise valid proposals:

> At the company I'm involved in now, we have a prioritised list of projects that will probably take the better part of two years to put in place. A few months ago when I joined, everyone was frustrated because they wanted it all done now and nothing was getting done.

Given the finance function's vital role in supporting operations, the state of the department's processes is another factor CFOs take into account when scrutinising investments. At Walmart International, the $130 billion division that runs the retailer's stores outside the United States, CFO Cathy Smith is trying to roll out a standardised accounting system across the unit's 26 countries and considering the creation of the group's first shared service centre for finance outside the United States. She says:

> In a couple of our markets we purposefully slowed our growth just so that we could build those foundational processes. Trying to grow a business rapidly on a weak foundation causes problems.

To a CFO's colleagues focused on their own priorities and pet projects, the investment-approval process can sometimes appear inscrutable. It is up to CFOs to communicate clear standards for business plans, including the benchmark financial and non-financial criteria, to help them understand that what is best for the company as a whole comes first.

Treasury and financing

Despite the depth and sophistication of modern capital markets, most companies rely on internal cash generation as their main source of capital. This is particularly true for smaller companies; a 2012 survey by CFO Research Services of finance executives at mid-market firms (those with annual revenues of $10m–500m) in the United States found more than three-quarters expected cash from ongoing operations to serve as their companies' primary source of growth capital in the future, well ahead of debt and equity financing.

Managing the sources of funds is an important responsibility of the CFO, supported by a treasury team that is usually centralised at company headquarters.[4] To raise capital, the finance chief's main options include wringing more cash out of operations, borrowing from banks, issuing debt in the capital markets or selling shares to investors. Former bankers are often found in corporate treasury teams, helping CFOs to weigh the costs and benefits of various financing options and scanning the capital markets for external threats and opportunities.

At the operational end of the funding spectrum, the CFO directs a company's working capital policies. This determines how quickly a company pays suppliers and collects from customers, and how much inventory it holds. The level of working capital is, in essence, the amount of cash trapped in operations, from uncollected bills to unused inventory gathering dust on warehouse shelves. REL reckons that some $2 trillion in "excess" working capital is languishing on the balance sheets of the largest companies in the United States and Europe. (The excess is calculated as the difference between top-quartile performers and the other three-quarters of firms.)

Close co-ordination is required between FP&A teams that work where cash is generated and the central treasury team that collects and monitors incoming funds. Incentives are also important to improving working capital efficiency. Linking sales commissions to when cash is received instead of when a sale is booked is one way to draw attention to collections. Incorporating working capital into financial targets, such as using return on capital employed instead of operating profit, is another way to attract attention to cash generation. The stick can be as useful as the carrot; Gerard van Kesteren, CFO of Kuehne & Nagel, a Swiss logistics company, introduced a policy that requires the CFO's approval for any contract with a payment term longer than 60 days. And whenever he receives such a request, "I say no". Squeezing more cash from receivables and payables requires an appreciation for customer and supplier relationships. Cut collection times or delay payments too aggressively, and the result could be lost sales or angry (or bankrupt) suppliers.

Historically, the biggest gains in working capital management have come from reducing inventories. Globalisation, specialisation and advances in supply chain management allow companies to operate with much lower levels of inventory than in the past. Still, excess inventory remains the area with the most scope for improvement, according to REL, accounting for more than 40% of the excess working capital "opportunity". Setting the appropriate level of inventory to meet customer demand without too much idle stock is a stern test for a CFO's forecasting abilities.

In part, the steady rise in cash on corporate balance sheets is the result of improved working capital performance (see Figure 3.2). The value of efficient operations and spare cash was made clear during the global financial crisis that began in 2008, when many external sources of funds dried up following the collapse of investment bank Lehman Brothers. The downturn marked a fundamental change in the way CFOs think about financing their businesses, according to Blythe McGarvie, a senior lecturer at Harvard Business School and former CFO of BIC, a French consumer-goods company, and Hannaford Brothers, a US retailer:

> *The CFO role reached an inflection point in 2008. People realised that funding could dry up. One of the key skills the CFO needs is finding and negotiating the right mix of funding by taking advantage*

FIG 3.2 **Balance sheet items of non-financial corporates in the United States**
% of total assets

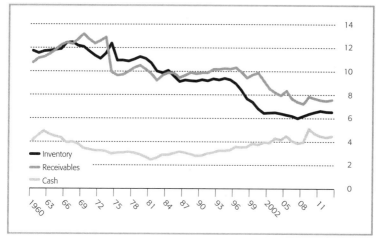

Source: US Federal Reserve

of interest rates today. Inflection points like this don't happen very often in a lifetime.

As stricken banks reined in lending and authorities in the United States and Europe cut interest rates to record lows (and pledged to keep them there for years), CFOs reassessed their companies' mix of debt and equity. Despite record levels of cash at Western firms, many took the opportunity to raise additional funds at historically low rates, if only to replace more expensive debt or extend repayment periods by issuing longer-term bonds.

Non-financial companies in the United States issued more than $1.3 trillion in bonds in 2012 with an average maturity of nearly 14 years per issue, according to Sifma, an industry group; ten years earlier, the comparable totals were $640 billion and eight years. European companies' traditional reliance on bank credit is also eroding. More than half of new debt issued by large companies in the first half of 2013 came from bonds placed in the capital market, according to Fitch Ratings, a credit-rating agency, compared with an average of 30% in 1999.

FIG 3.3 **Security issues at non-financial corporations in the United States**
Ratio of new bond issues to equity issues

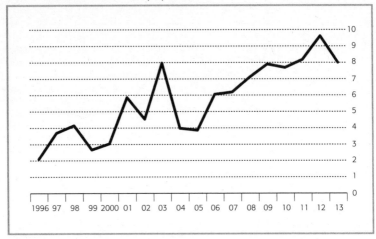

Source: US Federal Reserve

The preference for debt also reflects an aversion to equity (see Figure 3.3). On US exchanges there have been half as many initial public offerings (IPOs) in the ten years to 2012 as there were in the 1980s, to say nothing of the dotcom boom in the late 1990s. These days, when companies issue shares they often do so reluctantly; banks long resisted calls by regulators to raise equity to boost their capital cushions, while some of the highest profile IPOs in recent history, such as Google and Facebook, featured special classes of shares with limited voting powers, ensuring company founders can maintain control of their companies. (The CFO's relationship with investors, bankers and other market players is discussed in Chapter 4.)

At Apple, CFO Peter Oppenheimer faced a tricky financing challenge even as his company sat on $145 billion in cash and saw its popular products fly off the shelves, adding more cash to the pile each quarter. The episode was a good example of the creativity required to balance the competing interests inherent in a company's funding policy and balance-sheet strategy.

David Einhorn, a hedge fund manager, publicly criticised Apple in early 2013 for "hoarding" cash, calling for a more generous return to shareholders. After initial resistance, and perhaps chastened by its falling share price, Apple raised $17 billion in a heavily oversubscribed bond, the largest corporate issue on record at the time. The proceeds would help fund $100 billion in returns to shareholders by 2015 via share buy-backs and an increase to dividends.

Why did the debt-free, cash-rich company need to borrow at all? Two-thirds of its cash sat in foreign subsidiaries, facing a 35% tax if repatriated to the United States. If Apple used its foreign cash to pay for the buy-backs and dividend boost, it would trigger more than $9 billion in taxes. The bond, by contrast, will cost the company around $300m in annual interest. And since interest expense is deductible, Apple saves $100m a year on taxes as a result. As an exercise in placating restive investors with clever financial engineering, it was a success.

But market tides can shift quickly and unexpectedly. As a result, CFOs and their treasury teams need to revisit financing policies regularly. Improving economic conditions or the availability of external finance can distract managers from bolstering internal capital generation. And as the 2008 crisis showed, financial instruments and funding strategies that once seemed clever may prove calamitous in retrospect.

The pensions puzzle

Although few companies still offer employees final-salary pension schemes, the benefits promised in the past remain a concern. Indeed, with retirees living longer and interest rates near historic lows, pension obligations have soared. In extreme cases, the value of pension liabilities outstrips some companies' market capitalisation, a tail-wags-dog scenario.

When DBRS, a ratings agency, examined 461 of the largest defined-benefit corporate pension schemes in North America, Europe and Japan, it found an aggregate deficit of $536 billion at the end of 2012. This was the equivalent of pension assets covering only 78% of liabilities, dipping into the "danger zone" below the minimum prudent funding of 80%, the agency said.

For everyone except pension beneficiaries, investing in a business takes precedence over devoting funds to plug a deficit in the retirement plan. What is more, accounting rules in many countries require companies to report pension expenses as well as actuarial gains and losses at market values in their financial statements. This generates volatility and, in recent years, has depressed both profits and balance-sheet values in reported results. In the UK, for example, companies paid nearly £40 billion into defined-benefit schemes in 2012, compared with £14 billion in 2002 – even as membership in these schemes fell to 28% of employees in 2012, compared with 42% ten years earlier. Thus what was once administered in a sleepy corner of human resources is now near the top of the list of worries for some CFOs.

When interest rates rise from historic lows, this problem will diminish somewhat. Few expect deficits to go away any time soon, though, so some CFOs are taking drastic measures to remove the pension millstones weighing down company accounts. This means offering scheme members lump-sum buy-outs or offloading plans entirely to insurance companies (and paying them for the privilege). Despite large initial costs, the certainty of eliminating outsized, unpredictable obligations proved worth it for companies like EMI, Ford, GM and Verizon, all of which unloaded billions of dollars-worth of pension liabilities in 2012 and 2013.

Mergers and acquisitions

In the 20 years that he has worked for Essilor, the market leader in the global market for ophthalmic lenses, Laurent Vacherot has done a lot of deals. The company typically acquires 20–30 companies per year; in 2012 it took control of 24 firms, with deals as far afield as Laos, Togo and Tunisia. In and out of the finance department at the Paris-based group over the course of his career, including a stint as CFO from 2007 to 2010, Vacherot, now COO, says that the most important mergers and acquisitions (M&A) lesson he has learned is, simply, "take the time necessary".

This is not the first thing that comes to mind when describing the dealmaking process, with armies of advisers locked in high-stakes negotiations with tight deadlines and occasionally hostile rhetoric. The common wisdom that many, if not most, acquisitions end up destroying value also suggests that patience is not a common virtue. This could be a function of inexperience, as few companies are as active in M&A as Essilor. The excitement and emotions of a deal can cloud the judgment of otherwise rational executives; few activities appeal more to a CEO's empire-building instincts than M&A – the bigger and bolder, the better.

Thomas Meyding, a partner at CMS Hasche Sigle in Stuttgart, a law firm active in M&A advisory, says:

> The M&A team often gets lost in a transaction and just wants to get it done. CFOs should keep some distance in order to maintain objectivity and act as a counterweight to the deal team.

Boudewijn Beerkens, a former CFO of Wolters Kluwer, described his role at the Dutch publisher along these lines to a reporter at *FSI* magazine:

> It's up to the CEO to decide what to acquire. How and under what conditions is my responsibility. When it comes to agreeing a price and premium, I have the final say.

In this role, the CFO can wield effective veto power over a deal if the numbers do not stack up. Companies often consider far more acquisitions than they end up consummating; the finance chief's conservative nature is evident in this regard.

In late 2012, just over a year after Hewlett-Packard, a computer-maker, bought Autonomy, a UK software company, for $11.1 billion, it wrote down the value of the unit by a whopping $8.8 billion, claiming that the acquired company misrepresented a wide range of financial information. When a new CEO, Meg Whitman, joined HP after the deal was completed but before the write-down was announced, she said on a conference call with analysts that she was "surprised to find that due diligence and M&A reported to strategy instead of the chief financial officer". She suggested that this was a factor in the misguided, overvalued deal; she put CFO Cathie Lesjak in charge of dealmaking due diligence "right away before I knew any of this".

Acting as an objective arbiter of the wisdom of a deal is easier said than done. Smaller, "bolt-on" acquisitions are generally easier to negotiate and integrate, so they are much more common than the billion-dollar megadeals that capture headlines. Increasingly, however, smaller deals involve early-stage companies where know-how is more important than tangible assets. The shift away from manufacturing to services in the West is another reason more deals are now about "buying brains", according to Paul Finlan, a partner at Faegre Baker Daniels, a London-based law firm. Valuing these acquisitions is difficult, relying greatly on assumptions of how the new employees will perform under new ownership. Finlan explains:

> If they don't enjoy working for the new organisation, you can't force their brains to co-operate. After buying a manufacturing business, the machinery isn't going to lose its willpower and drive for you.

This highlights the importance of post-merger integration, an area sometimes overlooked by CFOs. In many ways, the work entailed in completing an acquisition – however demanding – is only the beginning of the M&A process. Without careful consideration of how the new company will mesh with the acquirer's operations, systems and culture, the expected benefits of a deal can quickly wash away as the time, effort and cost of integrating the purchase soak up company resources.

At Syngenta, a Swiss agribusiness company, a team dedicated to post-acquisition integration sits on the same level as the main M&A team, according to the CFO, John Ramsay. This unit considers the operational aspects of a deal well before an acquisition is completed. As such, it is a popular route for the development of finance staff, who gain broader skills on a compressed timeline during rotations through the integration unit.

The M&A watchword for Ramsay is "optionality". Given increasing competition for deals and the ever-present uncertainty of valuing targets, companies need to prepare for a wide range of potential scenarios, both before and after a deal is signed. For CFOs, this tests their financial judgment of the initial merits of a deal, leadership and communication skills if they feel the need to push back on colleagues in favour of an acquisition, and operational nous when the time comes to integrate a new purchase.

Because M&A is not a routine activity at most firms, maintaining an institutional memory of successes and failures – a dealmaking guidebook, of sorts – is often included among the CFO's other intelligence-gathering responsibilities. At Johnson & Johnson, a US health-care products company, this is down to a dedicated M&A finance team, as CFO Dominic Caruso described in a report produced by Booz & Company, a consultancy:

Once a year, we look back five years at all the acquisitions we've done. We try to extract lessons, because it doesn't always work the way you thought it would. Then we use those lessons either to fine-tune how we're integrating the acquisition or, at least, to put variables into our models that make them more precise.

At Essilor, one recent acquisition in Canada was 20 years in the making, says Vacherot. Needless to say, it takes strong convictions on the timing and price of an acquisition to keep a deal on the company radar for that long. This is a sign of the caution required with M&A, one of the riskier uses of a company's hard-won capital.

Risk management

Speaking of risk, for CFOs charged with protecting their companies from threats, the mantra "you can't manage what you can't measure" applies. In order to identify, prevent and mitigate all the risks that threaten a company, CFOs monitor an array of economic, financial and operational indicators.

For Timotheus Höttges of Deutsche Telekom, the goal of the executive team's "risk cockpit" is simple: to ensure "I never have the feeling that I have overlooked something". To this end, the dashboard includes 50 indicators for each of the markets the company operates in, including many with little obvious relevance to the telecoms industry. The Baltic Dry Index of sea-route shipping costs, for example, is one of the leading indicators the company tracks alongside a range of coincidental and lagging indicators.

"As CFO, I spend more time thinking about risks and the risk-register process than any of my executive colleagues," says Julian Metherell of Genel Energy. This is not down to "altruism", he notes.

Most risks have financial consequences, which brings them into the realm of the CFO. "If we don't produce 50,000 barrels of oil per day, my revenue guidance to investors will be wrong and I won't cover capex with free cash flow," he says. In addition, the board of directors' audit committee – the boardroom group that spends the most time with CFOs – is usually nominated to oversee a company's risk processes. Listed companies are also required to report extensively on the risks they face in their financial reports. For these reasons, CFOs and their finance teams are generally considered the "owners" of risk management systems.

As with the CFO's controlling and compliance duties, successful risk management is largely invisible to the rest of the company; threats are identified early, triggering corrective measures designed to cause minimal disruption. Most companies' risk radars, however, are only tuned to identify "known unknowns", to borrow a phrase from Donald Rumsfeld, a former US defence secretary. This is something Metherell is aware of:

> People tend to focus on risks that have the highest probability and the highest impact. The problem is that those are the things that people naturally worry about every day. The risks that tend to fundamentally damage and undermine companies are the high-impact, low-probability risks.

Thus it is the Rumsfeldian "unknown unknowns" that are, somewhat tautologically, the risks that catch companies off-guard. Not long ago, the break-up of the euro zone was practically unthinkable; it now sits prominently on any international company's list of major risks.

Genel Energy is, by its nature, a highly risky business. The oil exploration company operates fields primarily in the Kurdistan region of Iraq, with recent expansion into countries like Côte d'Ivoire and Somaliland. Metherell describes the mechanics of the company's risk register as "pretty straightforward":

> At Genel, we have 40–50 key risks. As an executive team, we go through the risk register every quarter. We identify the key risks and decide on the probability of those risks occurring – high, medium

*and low; the consequence were they to happen; and how we could
mitigate it. Each risk has an owner.*

Metherell owns all the purely financial risks. When the euro zone's
debt crisis peaked in mid-2012, the risk that one of the company's
banks could go bust rose in probability. The mitigating action was to
pull Genel's cash out of any bank with a credit rating below a certain
grade or a market-derived default risk above a set threshold, and buy
US Treasury bills instead. Executive risk owners must be judicious in
how actions cascade down into their teams; "It can't be complicated,"
Metherell says. In addition to monitoring credit ratings and market
indicators, a member of Genel's finance team rings each of its banks
every Monday to confirm that the company's cash is still there.

In a 2013 global survey of audit committee members by KPMG,
just over half were satisfied that their companies' risk management
processes addressed an "appropriately broad universe of risk"; a third
believed that risk processes were "dynamic enough to cope with a
rapidly changing environment"; and only a quarter thought their
risk-identification system looked "far enough into the horizon". On
this evidence, even if they plan for the best, good CFOs should be
imaginative in expecting the worst.

Of course, a certain amount of risk is inherent in any business.
Investors in Genel Energy seek exposure to the high-risk, high-reward
prospects in the frontier markets in which it operates. It would be safer
to drill in the North Sea, but the potential rewards – and associated
valuation of the company's shares – would not be as great. The risks
that investors cannot stomach, though, include the company losing
cash deposited in a bankrupt bank. In operations, a safety issue or
foreseeable technical fault would be similarly punished.

If an unforeseen event strikes, or a company's risk mitigation
strategy falls short, all is not lost. Actions taken while in recovery mode
can even enhance a company's reputation, according to the long-
running database of corporate crises by Oxford Metrica. Adjusted for
risk and market conditions, the consultancy measures the reaction to
a company's share price that it says is down purely to how it manages
following a crisis. Shares of the average "winner" rise above their
pre-crisis level within a month, gaining 15% within six months. The

typical "loser", by contrast, sees its shares drop by 10% in value almost immediately, sliding 15% lower within six months. When faced with calamity, "managerial awareness of what is required, and the courage to act accordingly, sends a strong signal of skill to investors," according to the researchers.

Prevention, of course, remains the primary objective of risk management. The foresight of the finance chief, accuracy of the finance team's forecasts and thoroughness of the scenario-planning process all contribute to a company's ability to anticipate and avoid unwanted risks.

Leadership

Even if it is a management truism, most CFOs say that people are the finance department's greatest assets. Given all the demands piled on finance chiefs, they are indeed only as good as the teams that support them. To this end, time devoted to developing financial talent in the lower ranks is far from selfless. Byron Pollitt, CFO of Visa, a multinational financial services corporation, described his mentoring role in a report published by Spencer Stuart, a recruitment company:

> Today, the demand on my time from non-finance people is very high and to create the most value in the organisation as CFO, I need to spend a disproportionate amount of time outside finance. That means I must have lieutenants who can run the finance side of the business with minimal direction from me, and what time I do give them is less about their day job and more about helping them with their own personal development.

Ten years ago, Pollitt hired staff based on "aptitude more than experience", given that the CFO had more time to train his reports on the details of their jobs. The teambuilding duties of the CFO, as leader of the finance function, are no less substantial today; the nature of how they are performed has changed, however, with more leadership responsibility pushed down to the lower management tiers in the department.

The structure of the contemporary finance department requires careful co-ordination at all levels. Whereas the monolithic finance department of old featured a traditional pyramidal hierarchy, finance today is a loose confederation of specialist silos. These are generally grouped into three categories: accounting and other transactional services, concentrated in a handful of sites; specialist functions like treasury, tax and M&A, located at the central and regional headquarters; and the financial analysis teams, partnered with operating managers and scattered widely throughout the business.

The CFO faces two main structural decisions. The first is how to drive down the cost of delivering routine transactional processes. Placing shared service centres in low-cost countries is one way to cut labour costs. The Hackett Group estimates there will be a net decline in finance jobs of more than 40% between 2002 and 2016 at large companies in Europe and the United States, thanks to a combination of productivity improvements and "offshoring". Outsourcing the transactional functions entirely, meanwhile, converts the fixed cost of labour into a variable one, governed by service-level agreements with a third-party outsourcing firm.[5]

The second decision is how to draw the reporting lines for finance's dispersed business-partnering roles. To ensure greater control, a so-called "solid line" means that staff report up through finance regardless of where they are based, emphasising their allegiance is to finance first and business partners second. Non-financial managers may dislike this, seeing the finance colleagues dispatched to support them as aloof or conflicted. A "dotted-line" relationship, whereby business-unit finance managers report to general managers instead of via finance channels, makes it clear that they are there to support the business, but heightens the risk of compliance breakdowns if they succumb to pressure from non-financial bosses. The truly intrepid employ a matrix reporting system, making finance managers serve multiple masters simultaneously, a tricky balancing act.

Companies in a defensive, cost-cutting mode are more liable to maintain solid-line reporting systems, while growth-oriented, entrepreneurial firms are likely to feature dotted-line relationships. Whatever the case, it is up to the CFO to foster a sense of community throughout the finance function, motivating and developing staff to tackle their ever-growing responsibilities.

This begins with recognition. At PayPal, a fast-growing online payment processor based in Silicon Valley, CFO Patrick Dupuis says, "It is my obligation as a CFO to get as much respect for the back office as we do for our developers."

Andre Alexander has served as CFO of several non-profit organisations, including FARE, a food-allergy awareness group, Special Olympics and the Jane Goodall Institute. Front-office workers at these organisations routinely receive plaudits, given the noble nature of their work; for the back-office finance staff to receive their due, Alexander acts as their "chief cheerleading officer" from his perch on the executive committee.

Of course, kind words can only go so far – the development of next-generation financial talent requires action. The goal is clear, according to Andy Halford, CFO of Vodafone, a UK mobile telecoms company, speaking to Ernst & Young for a report about finance leadership:

> The perfect finance person has mastered the technical, they're strong on the interpersonal, they have worked in different countries and done operational roles and seen finance from the other side of the fence.

This is a tall order. It is no wonder, then, that in a 2013 survey of British finance chiefs by Robert Half, a recruitment firm, more than half of respondents had no succession plan in place, with the most common reason a "lack of existing internal talent". There is a certain amount of executive hubris in this claim – après mois, le déluge – as there are several examples of companies that successfully churn out top financial talent below the CFO ranks.

In the backgrounds of CFOs at large US firms, four companies stand out. In early 2013, CCL Search, a recruitment firm, counted nearly 130 CFOs serving at companies with more than $1 billion in revenues who spent time at GE, Honeywell, PepsiCo and General Motors. This is not a coincidence, as each firm is well-known for its financial talent development programmes.

At GE, fresh-out-of-university, high-potential finance hires are put through the company's famed Financial Management Programme, a two-year plan that features four six-month assignments in a variety of roles. From there, it is common to join the Corporate Audit Staff, another two-year plan (with up to six rotations) on which employees act as an internal auditor at disparate businesses. Later, more senior financial assignments typically run for two-year stints. Needless to say, in fairly short order these workers are exposed to a huge variety of financial activities, which is common at the other "academy companies", according to Christopher Langhoff, managing partner at CCL Search (and a former PepsiCo finance staffer):

> *They tend to have broad experience. They've been given more opportunities at younger ages to run things. They have more experience in senior roles, because those companies take a chance on them. These are up-and-out kind of places – you don't stay long at Pepsi or GE without producing.*

Growing pains

The concept of "best practice" is not often as universally applicable as the management consultants insist. In developing countries, in particular, although the responsibilities of CFOs are much the same as in mature markets, the emphasis can differ significantly. The devil, as they say, is in the details.

Yan Huiping joined Home Inns, a Shanghai-based hotelier, in 2010 as CFO. She spent the previous 11 years at GE, serving in a variety of finance roles in Asia and the United States.

A key advantage her company enjoys over Western hotel chains is a higher risk tolerance, Yan says. There are few better training grounds for finance executives than GE, but the CFO was still sure to "keep an open mind" when she joined Home Inns. Adapting to the local circumstances, she says, requires a focus on "substance over form". The idiosyncrasies of property ownership in China, for example, mean that the company sometimes deals with leaseholders whose documents proving ownership are construction permits or fire-inspection certificates. A Western company's rules might preclude them from dealing with owners without a certain kind of title.

In other areas, Yan found the application of rules at Home Inns far too strict. The company's NASDAQ listing exposes it to US securities law and corporate governance rules, including the onerous Sarbanes-Oxley Act. The company applied these rules a bit too exactingly, with many layers of attestations required for even minor transactions. With "redundancies, checks and balances everywhere", the CFO says the net effect was both slower decision-making and, paradoxically, a reduced sense of responsibility since compliance tasks were so pervasive that they became rote. A streamlined new system limits sign-offs to a more prudent number of senior managers.

Getting her team out of their "finance pigeonhole" is a challenge. Finding qualified staff to begin with is a struggle, a common frustration in China and many other emerging markets. While at GE, Yan noted that the finance department at one Chinese firm the group acquired was cut from more than 200 to less than 30.

Yan's work at Home Inns can be "more spread out and at a much lower level" than during her time at GE. CFOs at emerging-market firms generally exert less influence on overall company strategy than at developed-market firms, although the demands on finance departments are equally weighty. In a survey of CFOs in China by Deloitte, a professional services firm, respondents cited "strategic ambiguity" as their top concern alongside the lack of qualified staff.

Certain aspects of the CFO's role in emerging markets recall the function's stature decades ago in the West. But other difficulties facing CFOs in developing countries would be welcomed by CFOs in the West, not least the "problem" of managing breakneck growth. Since its founding in 2002, Home Inns has amassed a portfolio of more than 2,000 hotels across China, generating around $1 billion in annual revenue. At its current pace, it opens a new hotel every day.

Building well-rounded staff takes concerted effort, given the increasingly specialised nature of finance roles. Years ago, an employee could gain exposure to various transactional, specialist and commercial-facing roles in the same office, if not in the same position; today, functions are often split into dedicated teams in far-flung locations. Rotations are crucial: if staff get stuck in silos, they are unlikely to gain the experience necessary to rise to the senior ranks. As a result, according to Richard Cardillo, leader of the finance transformation practice at Hackett, some companies avoid the all-or-nothing approach to offshoring and outsourcing, even if it sacrifices efficiency. By outsourcing only, say, 90% of routine accounting activities, retained functions can serve as internal training grounds for finance staff, ensuring a greater breadth of experience for staff on rotations.

It may sound gruelling to older generations, but young financial talent expect frequent, wide-ranging rotations. A large survey of finance employees born after 1980 by ACCA, a professional association, and Mercer, a consultancy, found that more than half expected to move from their current role within two years. They also split 60–40 between those seeking broad business experience that includes non-financial roles, even if it means slower progression in seniority, and those looking for a classic finance path that emphasises traditional roles and entails a quicker rise up the management ladder.

Identifying these aspirations early on is important. Santiago Fernández Valbuena, former CFO of Telefónica, a Spanish telecoms company, and now running its Latin American operations, told researchers at Ernst & Young:

> The kind of people you want to do auditing, accounting and reporting will not possess the same leadership skills you need for someone to be a successful group CFO.

He likens this to the difference between sumo wrestlers and marathon runners: "They are both athletes but they will fare poorly at each other's sport."

At Shell, fateful conversations with finance employees begin after 5–10 years of experience, usually around age 30. In an ICAEW report, CFO Simon Henry says:

> We can discuss where their preferences may actually lie and emphasise that it's okay to specialise or to develop in a more general sense, provided you accept the capabilities you need to demonstrate and the fact that you can't go backwards once you have made a particular choice.

There is a risk, he adds, that in the absence of frank assessments of team members' skills, the mix of financial talent at a company can become imbalanced:

> One of the challenges we have is that too many finance staff aspire to be business partners ... We have to find ways to inspire and

*motivate people to run the engine very well, not always be thinking
about building a new engine. It remains one of the challenges in
developing staff, because I think that in order to carry out more
senior roles you have to have done both earlier in your career.
There's too much incitement, partly in the profession as well, that
business partnering is where all the kudos is.*

At rival energy company BP, personal technical development
activities for financial staff are supported by the dedicated internal
BP Financial University. Its faculties offer more than 300 courses,
from entry-level courses on cash optimisation to the capstone CFO
Excellence Programme, focusing on the company's top 250 financial
managers and emphasising their "distinct role as champions of
integrity and compliance, while leading assured change, and playing
a broader role as a leader in the business," according to the company.

The transition from demonstrating technical competence to
becoming an effective leader is a watershed moment in any finance
career. In 2009, BP introduced a policy in which promotions
from professional status – generally employees with at least ten
years' experience – to the next level of leadership is subject to an
independent technical assessment panel. The CFO advocating for the
person's promotion cannot sit on this panel, which comprises various
financial experts from elsewhere in the firm. This panel evaluates
the technical skills of the candidate, wielding veto power over the
promotion if they are not satisfied. This sends a signal that "your
technical skills are valued by BP and will be tested, so invest in them
wisely and continuously," says Andrew Grant, head of BP Financial
University.

In terms of rotations, evidence suggests that international
experience is the most effective way to boost a finance employee's
skills. In an assessment of more than 2,000 finance staff at 75
companies, CEB, an advisory company, found that the biggest gap in
employees' level of skills was found between those who had been
on a variety of geographic rotations and those who stayed put in
a country. The effectiveness of rotations within finance, between
divisional and central roles, and in non-financial roles was also
apparent, but the improvements were smaller.

Rotations are about more than honing functional skills. Lawrence Litowitz, a partner at SCA Group, a recruitment firm, and former CFO at several public and private companies, credits the "million-dollar mistakes" that a mentor let him make as a key factor in the "multimillion-dollar achievements" he was later able to achieve. Good leadership is "in abundance when things are going well, but you can only test it when things go wrong," notes Ramsay of Syngenta. As well as the ability to turn around a division financially, how well subordinates rate a manager's stewardship under stress can be an important signal that the person is potential CFO material.

Ajit Kambil runs the "Transition Lab", a one-day programme for new CFOs, at Deloitte. After more than 200 of these engagements, one of the common misconceptions he sees among incoming finance chiefs relates to the quality of their teams:

> I get serial CFOs as well as first timers. The first-time promotees generally think that the talent in their organisation is just fine. But after we have talked through priorities, they realise that the team may not be able to get them there. The serials know that it's never easy to restructure an organisation, especially the congenial "B" and "C" players, and they are more willing to engage talent aggressively.

Measures to address talent-development issues should be prominent on a new CFO's 180-day plan, says Kambil. The focus should not then fade, of course, as the promotion of effective, autonomous leaders throughout a CFO's senior team is a crucial factor in the finance chief's success. With so many CFOs themselves earning promotions to chief executive roles, since the finance function will continue to serve as a crucial source of support, they had better leave it in good shape.

4 Relationships: colleagues and partners, friends and foes

BY ITS NATURE, finance is a technical field with obscure jargon understood almost exclusively by its practitioners. When CFOs interact with their teams, they are free to employ this arcane language. But to fulfil their crucial role as business partners outside the finance function, they need a different approach. According to Lawrence Litowitz of SCA Group:

> You have to be able to put yourself in someone else's shoes to see what they need. They don't tell you what they need, and they don't necessarily know what you can give them.

Like any good leader, CFOs are most effective when they adapt their knowledge and influence to suit the audience. Given their central position, the demands on a CFO's time come from a wide range of constituencies outside of the finance department. This chapter describes some of the CFO's relationships with colleagues and partners, both inside and outside a company.

Chief executive officer

The CFO's most important relationship, without question, is with the CEO. In a 2010 survey of Fortune 500 CFOs with tenures of more than six years by the Korn/Ferry Institute, building a trusted partnership with the CEO was cited as a first-time CFO's most critical factor for success. This surpassed an operational understanding of the business, dealing with investors and all the other responsibilities that come when making the step up to finance chief.

More often than not, the top executive duo is defined by their complementary skillsets. If the CEO is the heart of a company, the CFO is its head. The chief executive provides the passion, the CFO the pragmatism. Less happily, the CFO is sometimes cast in the role of goon in a good cop-bad cop gambit, charged with cutting costs while the CEO extols exciting plans for growth. Whatever the nature of the partnership, it is crucial for the CFO to forge a productive relationship with the CEO.

In a survey of CEOs and CFOs, John Graham, Campbell Harvey and Manju Puri, professors at Duke University, identified noteworthy differences in the way the executives made capital-spending decisions. Both CEOs and CFOs gave the net present value and timing of cash flows similar scores in terms of their importance. Outside these orthodox measures, however, the other reasons for allocating resources receive significantly different emphasis. CEOs are much more likely to cite "gut feel" as an important consideration; CFOs are more likely to factor in the previous return of a similar project. CEOs also tend to weigh the proposing manager's reputation more highly when allocating capital; perhaps because of this, CFOs cite "corporate politics" more often than CEOs as a determinant of spending decisions.

The yin-and-yang nature of the CEO-CFO relationship works best when there is mutual regard for the other's position. In practice, this puts the onus on CFOs to establish their independence. "You need to have enough stature and respect from the chief executive that you can say 'no'," asserts Peter Harris, who has served as finance chief at a number of media and marketing firms in the UK. "It's not blind allegiance."

Indeed, given the CFO's fiduciary duties, blind allegiance can lead to trouble. In a 2011 study by Mei Feng, Weili Ge, Shuqing Luo and Terry Shevlin of more than 70 US companies caught manipulating their accounts, one of the biggest differences between firms that cooked the books and those that did not was the size of share-price-linked bonuses awarded to CEOs. The incentive packages for CFOs at manipulating and non-manipulating companies were similar enough to fail the tests for statistical significance. As a result, the researchers concluded:

CFOs are involved in material accounting manipulations because they succumb to pressure from CEOs, rather than because they seek immediate personal financial benefit from their equity incentives.

Higher turnover of CFOs ahead of the discovery of accounting manipulations also suggests that standing up to a CEO bent on fiddling earnings often costs finance chiefs their jobs.

Culture clash

In a speech to members of the Financial Executives Institute in 1963, William Cary, then chairman of the US securities regulator, urged the CFOs in the audience to resist pressure from CEOs to engage in accounting "chicanery" to flatter earnings. "In some cases you may say you cannot control your chief executive officer – a 'salesman at heart'," he said.

The differences in personalities between CFOs and CEOs have long been observed.[1] A trio of professors at Duke University set out to measure this empirically, giving psychometric tests to around 2,500 CFOs and CEOs. They found that, yes, CEOs are more optimistic than CFOs. In fact, they are more optimistic than just about everyone; 80% of the CEO sample was classified as "very optimistic", which the academics note is "well above the mean in the psychology literature norms". CFOs are not the gloomy bunch they are sometimes typecast as – 65% are classified as very optimistic – but they are not nearly as cheerful as their bosses. (The results, published in the *Journal of Financial Economics* in 2013, also showed that US executives tend towards higher optimism than their European counterparts, regardless of the position they hold.)

Similar results are evident in other studies, such as one by Deloitte that sought to categorise CFOs and CEOs at a sample of companies into one of four personality types: driver, guardian, integrator and pioneer. The most common CFO-CEO combination is a driver CFO and pioneer CEO. Drivers are characterised as analytical, logical and pragmatic, while pioneers are adventurous, creative and spontaneous.

According to the Duke researchers, higher CEO optimism is linked with more short-term debt and acquisition activity. This makes it important for the CFO to act as a balance to hard-charging chief executives, which indeed appears to be the case according to Deloitte's observations. Just over half of finance chiefs are classified as drivers, a "decisive, direct, tough-minded" character that translates a CEO's vision into a practical reality, without compromising their ethics if the boss asks them to get "creative" in the wrong sort of way.

Disagreements over strategy, rather than outright illegality, are much more common between CFOs and CEOs. At most companies, these disputes take place behind closed doors, with the top two executives presenting a united front in public. Michael Clarke, finance chief at ADAS, a UK environmental consultancy, describes his approach with the CEOs he has worked for over a long career at listed and private companies, large and small:

> If there were any issues where we disagreed with each other, we disagreed outside board meetings. I remember the feedback from one director was, "I wish they wouldn't look as though they had pre-prepared everything prior to the meeting or would argue from time to time." What the directors didn't see was the arguing.

Of course, the CFO's subordinate position to the CEO can make these arguments a somewhat delicate affair. But the growing power and influence of CFOs gives them a lot more leverage in these discussions than before. Moshe Banai and Philip Tulimieri, professors at Baruch College's Zicklin School of Business, reckon that a "partnership of equals" is now emerging at many companies:

> The global corporation to which business is evolving will be led by a duopoly: two equal partners, with equal accountability, authority and access to the people, processes and technology of the business will now run the organisation. They would be simply the obverse and reverse of the same coin – they would be interchangeable and complementary parts. They would speak with the same voice to the stakeholders and be equally charged with achieving the corporation's strategic objectives.

In this arrangement, the CFO and CEO "complement each other so well that it will be seamless to all but the inner circle of subordinates," Banai and Tulimieri conclude.

Indeed, open clashes between the CFO and CEO are rare, and almost always end badly for the finance chief. Joe Kaeser was one of the few to buck this trend in July 2013. A 33-year veteran at Siemens, a German conglomerate, the CFO of six years saw his counterpart in the executive suite, CEO Peter Löscher, ousted after a series of quarterly profit shortfalls and missed revenue targets. According to reports, the finance chief was not necessarily a bystander, as detailed by *Der Spiegel*:

> *Siemens has always had confident CFOs. But Kaeser has been so openly critical that some at the company have already eyed him with suspicion in the past. Others call him authentic. Kaeser himself says: "It's time for the CEO to tell us where we're going. The CFO's job is to ask how we're going to get there."*

Exactly two weeks after this conversation, everything had changed. Löscher was ousted and Kaeser was chosen as his successor. When asked whether he played a role in Löscher's ousting, Kaeser was circumspect:

> *All I have done is occasionally point out that such targets need to be backed up with substance. That should be perfectly acceptable, in a company led by an executive board that encourages open debate. A key role is played in this respect by the chief financial officer, because it is his task to inspect allocation of funding. Peter Löscher and I are no doubt very different types, but both of us, and the executive board, have been entrusted to lead Siemens to success.*

After Kaeser stepped up from CFO to CEO at Siemens, he emphasised the conservatism that one would expect from a former finance chief, asserting to a conference call with analysts that "we have been trying to achieve too much too quickly" and noting that his top priority was "to calm our enterprise and to stabilise its internal organisation".

Adversity need not lead to the break-up of CEO-CFO duos. Indeed, it can strengthen them, according to Jesper Brandgaard of Novo Nordisk. He was appointed CFO in November 2000, the same time as the CEO, Lars Rebien Sørensen. A formative moment in their relationship came 18 months later, when a profit warning knocked 50% off the company's share price. "We had to revise our plans and face the music," Brandgaard recalls. The CFO's ability to handle the tricky task of crafting a communications plan to placate irate investors put him in the CEO's good graces:

> It was at one of those meetings when Lars realised that I was able to express myself clearly in ways that created reasonable expectations. That was a significant change in the way we worked. We have both characterised that profit warning as a blessing in disguise. We learned that we had complementary competencies.

In the 13 years since Brandgaard and Sørensen took over as CFO and CEO, Novo Nordisk's share price has risen more than sevenfold.

Another perspective on the CFO-CEO relationship comes from executives who have served in both positions. Before joining Prudential, Jackie Hunt served as finance chief at Standard Life and Aviva under CEOs with previous CFO experience. Having sat on the other side of the table, these chief executives appreciated a CFO who stood up to them, she says. "They don't take it personally."

Before Jim Buckle became CFO at Wiggle, a UK-based online sports-goods retailer, he was managing director at Lovefilm, a DVD-by-mail and video-on-demand provider acquired by Amazon in 2011. In making the step up from CFO to CEO shortly after the takeover, he questioned the necessity of a bona fide CFO, given that the firm, by becoming a division in a much larger group, would cede many financial responsibilities to its new parent company. Instead, he could rely on his financial acumen and the existing accounting and financial analysis specialists who were part of his team when he was CFO. Or so he thought:

> What I discovered is that the CFO is hugely valuable. Running a business can be a lonely place, and the CFO performs a really important function by being the person that the CEO can bounce ideas off and be challenged by. You need people who will tell you how it is, but not in a destructive way.

Some healthy tension between the CFO and CEO is acceptable,

even encouraged. But once decisions are made, whether a finance chief's input is accepted or not, the CFO needs to support the CEO and make sure actions are implemented in a financially prudent way. If a CFO cannot accept the CEO's chosen direction, the main alternatives are resignation or a high-stakes gamble on persuading the board to side against the chief executive.

Board of directors

Although the CFO's closest day-to-day working relationship is with the CEO, the stakes are often higher during interactions with the board. Directors look to CFOs for an independent assessment of corporate performance and priorities, which can put them in a tough spot – between the boss and the boss's bosses. Balancing these competing interests requires tact and diplomacy.

In the minds of directors, it is common to hear the finance chief described as the board's "conscience". This is, in effect, a demonstration of the CFO's role as the level-headed pragmatist in the executive team. The CEO's assessments and plans obviously take priority, but the CFO's ability to provide board members with a deeper understanding of the risks and alternatives to these plans is no less important. (It also goes without saying that the CFO must forge strong bonds with the members of the audit committee, generally the most important subcommittee of the board, given its oversight of accounting, risk and compliance.)

Christopher Butler and Karen Quint, recruiters at Spencer Stuart, describe the CFO's increasingly prominent position vis-à-vis the board of directors:

> CFOs have become a second set of eyes that directors should use in deliberations over the future course of their companies. CFOs can increase transparency for the board and raise issues that otherwise might go unnoticed. Especially in companies with international operations, it is hard for directors to grasp component parts and how they interrelate. CFOs help clarify business models, draw the maps of activities, and provide a deeper sense of how a business actually works, its risks and opportunities.

A CFO's work for the board begins well in advance of the actual meetings with directors. In the same way that they assemble and vet the information created for investors, CFOs are often involved in preparing the supporting material for board meetings. This gives them scope to influence the agenda and tone of these meetings, as well as demonstrating their command of a company's key performance drivers. Directors, particularly non-executive directors, deal almost exclusively in big-picture strategy, so a careful synthesis of information that is detailed enough to answer their questions, but not so exhaustive as to overwhelm them with material, is required.

Kevin Rakin, a pharmaceutical industry veteran, has served as CFO, CEO and director at several companies. In his capacity as a board member, he told CFO.com that preparation is what marks the best CFOs from the rest:

> Among all the companies whose boards I've been on, one CFO stands out. You get [from this CFO] a monthly report that has corralled all the other leaders in the business and puts their opinions into one written communication. When there's just a board meeting once every three months where you're touching base on the phone, you don't always get a holistic sense of things.

When he first joined XL Group, a global insurance company, CFO Peter Porrino reached out to the heads of the audit and risk committees on the company's board, suggesting that they speak a week before every board meeting. This was not something his predecessors did, and it has proved valuable in making the meetings with directors go more smoothly. Porrino explained his approach to the *Wall Street Journal*:

> I've found that having a relationship and an ability to communicate in advance of a meeting what the issues are likely to be make all the difference in the world during the meeting.

A good relationship with the CEO and directors makes for productive, substantive board meetings. Sometimes, however, if disagreements between the CFO and CEO cannot be reconciled, the board can serve as an outlet for the finance chief to lobby for support. This is not without considerable risks, since surprises are generally unwelcome in board meetings, and a feud between the top two executives would rank as a big surprise.

The showdown between CEO and CFO at Hewlett-Packard in 2012 is a good example. The CEO, Léo Apotheker, and the CFO, Cathie Lesjak, were reportedly at odds over missed revenue targets, but things came to a head when they disagreed over the price the chief executive was willing to pay for the ill-fated acquisition of software company Autonomy (discussed in Chapter 3). According to an account in *Fortune* of the fateful board meeting when the deal was discussed, the CFO made her feelings clear:

> With no warning to Apotheker, Lesjak made an impassioned case against the acquisition before the board. "I can't support it," she told the directors, according to a person who was present. "I don't think it's a good idea. I don't think we're ready. I think it's too expensive. I'm putting a line down. This is not in the best interests of the company." Directors were shaken. Lesjak was considered a voice of sobriety, and here she was on the verge of insubordination, directly resisting a key element of her boss's strategy.

Although the company went through with the deal, it soon came to regret it. The CEO was dismissed after only ten months in the job and the CFO, a 24-year company veteran, remained in her post.

The trust and credibility that a CFO builds with directors is hard won; it requires painstaking preparation and finely tuned interpersonal skills. The CFOs who demonstrate their worth are given pride of place around the boardroom table, helping directors craft a company's strategic agenda. The others are merely in the room.

Family affair

The politics of the boardroom can be complex at the best of times. The intrigue is compounded when board members are also family members.

"Gaining and sustaining the trust of the family is an ongoing challenge," says Don Janezic, CFO of Bigelow Tea, a $150m US drinks company now run by the second generation of the Bigelow family. Janezic has been finance chief at the family-owned firm since 1987, and is one of its longest-serving non-family managers. As such, his thoughts on establishing credibility with directors are applicable for all types of company.

"I never try to endear myself to one family member over another," he says, stressing that independence is one of a CFO's most important assets. "Other family members see that and begin to respect it." Consistency and continuity are things that every CFO strives for, and qualities that all board members appreciate.

Sales and marketing

There is plenty of tact required when a CFO deals with superiors like the chief executive or board of directors, and nuance is necessary to manage and motivate subordinates in the finance team. In some ways, the CFO's relationship with fellow functional managers can be even more fraught; the finance chief usually outranks other functional heads but leads a department that is intended to serve them.

Nowhere is this more apparent than with the sales and marketing teams, the creative, client-facing "front-office" functions. The contrast with the rigid, transactional nature of finance's many "back-office" tasks can be stark. Experienced salespeople and marketers often argue that their work is more art than science, which rankles data-driven finance chiefs. Finding a middle ground is key, establishing measures that gauge the effectiveness of sales and marketing efforts without introducing unnecessary barriers to exercising the creative licence that can be crucial in attracting and retaining customers.

Like most aspects of modern business, the trend is towards more rather than less measurement. Tammy Smulders, managing director of SCB Partners, a London-based marketing consultancy, confirms this is the case with what were previously "wishy-washy" decisions:

> Gut feeling used to govern a lot of things. Now, it's just too risky to let people go on random whims like that. There are a lot of new hoops to jump through.

When it comes to sales and marketing, these new hurdles include a host of measures that aim to quantify the customer journey, from how much it costs to acquire a customer to the success of converting leads to sales and the lifetime value of certain customer segments. This tends to favour "inside" sales teams – a centralised function using phone calls, e-mails and the like – because it is easier to collect and observe data on their activities. The traditional "outside" sales representative pounding the pavement is still necessary, but the higher costs and lower transparency inherent in this method make it less attractive to numbers-driven finance departments.

Marketing, too, must justify its campaigns with a greater degree of financial savvy than in the past. The old adage attributed to an American retail pioneer, John Wanamaker – "Half the money I spend on advertising is wasted; the trouble is I don't know which half" – still rings true today, but the rise of the internet, social media and other more measurable channels makes a company's marketing efforts much more sophisticated than in Wanamaker's day.

The wealth of data now available on once-mysterious sales and marketing activities is improving the relationships between these functions and the CFO. Still, it is never easy to draw a direct line from a marketing campaign with ambiguous aims to cash in the bank. In a book aimed at marketers by David Stewart, Allen Weiss and Roy Young, a trio of professors and practitioners, this is addressed in a chapter entitled "Forge a Friendship with Your CFO":

> The more you can show how your marketing efforts produce cash flow, the greater influence you'll have with the CFO. To demonstrate this link, you need to understand how your organisation generates cash, demonstrate an entrepreneur's zeal for producing cash, and promote marketing's role as a cash generator throughout your organisation.

The CFO's relationship with sales and marketing teams is not a one-way street, with finance simply demanding more and more measures from frontline colleagues to justify their activities. Increasingly, CFOs themselves are playing an active role in the sales process, particularly for large clients in business-to-business industries. When he was CFO of Safety-Kleen, an environmental-services company, Jeff Richard went on the occasional customer visit with sales colleagues, as he explained to CFO.com:

> *At first, the sales folks don't like that at all ... But eventually they*
> *see that if they've had a hard time cracking a potential customer,*
> *as a CFO I might be able to get into that company's C-suite more*
> *easily. And commissions aren't part of my compensation. The sales*
> *manager will get the commission.*

This is becoming more common as CFOs are given outright responsibility for regional or divisional business units in addition to their finance responsibilities. It also helps promote a better understanding between the front- and back-office camps.

There is a risk in pushing the CFO's sales responsibility too far, lest it compromise the risk and control functions that are more central to the finance chief's remit. Frequent intervention by finance chiefs also risks resentment among sales and marketing staff. (But as Richard points out, "That's one of the good things about being the CFO. It's hard for them to say no.") Although conflicts can arise when the lines between the front and back office blur, on the whole a deeper co-operation between the functions, if managed carefully, is beneficial for all involved.

Human resources

The touchy-feely image of human resources is almost diametrically opposed to the stereotypical impression of the cold, calculating CFO. But CFOs ignore the emotional aspects of employee morale and motivation at their peril. Not everyone is motivated solely by money, and fostering a company culture can require investments that are not easily defined.

According to a rather devastating survey by the Economist Intelligence Unit in 2012, CFOs do not think highly of their colleagues in HR. Around two-thirds of finance chiefs say the head of HR is not of the same calibre as other C-level executives, and a similar share believes HR executives do not understand their businesses well enough. Tellingly, only a fifth of CEOs felt the same way about HR managers.

Considering that many chief executives come from finance backgrounds, this suggests a change of heart on the importance of HR issues when stepping up to the top job. Paul Sparrow, director of the Centre for Performance-led HR at Lancaster University, told the Economist Intelligence Unit:

> CFOs can rely on the power of their position and the centrality of finance to all things, so they might not be so attuned to other sources of power at the board level.

One of the biggest areas of disagreement between CFOs and HR directors revolves around the measurement of human capital. Employee surveys, assessments of aptitude and other "soft" measures are sometimes difficult to link with hard financial data, so finance and HR teams need to collaborate to identify the relationships between people and profit. Valerie Rainey, CFO of INTTRA, a New Jersey-based e-commerce company, says:

> In my experience the organisation views human capital analytics as more credible when they are jointly developed by HR and finance. In this way the organisation can maximise the expertise and skills that the management accountant can bring to this area.

If they can agree on the right measures, finance and HR can work together to establish effective incentive schemes, marrying HR's understanding of motivation and morale with finance's grip on business strategy. Whereas introducing bonuses based on, say, working capital performance might make sense from a financial perspective, CFOs cannot lose sight of the impact this could have on employee satisfaction. HR is a useful sounding board in this regard, and also in devising measures of employee engagement to feature on a CFO's dashboard of key performance indicators.

Carlo Ferro, CFO of STMicroelectronics, a multinational semiconductor manufacturer, says:

> Together with HR, we devise incentive schemes that enhance the cohesiveness of the organisation and see to it that our people are engaged. This is a classical interaction between finance and HR.

Information technology

CFOs owe advances in technology much of the credit for propelling them to their current prominence. The tedious, manually intensive work that it once took to compile accounts and create financial reports is a thing of the past thanks to IT. Few corporate functions have been transformed as comprehensively by technology as finance.

Still, the CFO's relationship with technology is often an uneasy one. Around half of all chief information officers (CIOs) report to the CFO, according to various surveys. CFOs appear to rate their ability to manage the IT function more highly than those working in it; a 2008 survey of European executives by CFO Research Services found that while more than 70% of CFOs thought that their most recent collaboration with CIOs was successful, just under 40% of CIOs felt the same.

This tension is often a result of the perceived aims of a company's technology strategy. By most accounts, the average firm spends around three-quarters of its IT budget on maintaining existing systems, with the remainder devoted to new initiatives. Wringing more value from a company's current systems is not as sexy as rolling out cutting-edge new technologies, which can be a source of conflict between a CFO mindful of costs and a CIO eager to upgrade to the latest and greatest technologies.

CFOs maintain a natural scepticism of big and bold IT projects, based on the tendency for them to go wrong. According to research by McKinsey, large IT projects – defined as having a budget of more than $15m – typically run 45% over budget, 7% over time and deliver less than half of the predicted value. The longer a project is scheduled to last, the more likely it is to blow its budget; with each additional year boosting the probability of missing its target by 15%. The consultancy added up $66 billion in cost overruns in the 5,400 IT projects it studied, which it points out is more than the GDP of Luxembourg.

This is not to say that CFOs shun technology. Quite the opposite. Advances in data-gathering software, virtualisation of systems that no longer require costly hardware to run and a host of related developments make it difficult for CFOs to pass up new opportunities to boost the sophistication of measuring corporate performance.

Increasingly granular and comprehensive data help finance bolster its reporting capabilities and, more importantly, its ability to anticipate risks and produce forward-looking forecasts.

Given the rapid pace of change in the IT world, simply keeping up-to-date consumes a big share of a company's investments. Most finance chiefs say they wish that their companies spent a larger share of the IT budget on whizzy new initiatives instead of mundane maintenance, but in their role as risk managers they know that giving the CIO a blank cheque and limited oversight is a recipe for trouble.

What's more, the benefits of modern technology are increasingly difficult to quantify ahead of time, unlike the time and money saved by switching from paper ledgers to their digital equivalents. "Business intelligence" software sounds good, but justifying the investment in these systems in terms of predictable outcomes requires a leap of faith. Don Janezic, CFO of Bigelow Tea, describes the finance chief's complicated relationship with technology today:

> Not that long ago we would measure the effectiveness of technology using a specific measure of the increase in productivity and efficiency. We could directly relate it to something else happening. Now, you cannot quantify it but you know without it you would be missing out.
>
> It's no longer black and white. That is a hard thing for CFOs. You need to be a little more intuitive and less judgmental.

Think big

The promise of "big data" generates excitement among most executives, but CFOs are perhaps the keenest. As the conduit through which most corporate information flows, the idea of tapping ever-larger pools of data is music to the finance department's collective ears. "When you make the hidden visible, interesting things can happen," says Esa Tihilä, chief executive of Basware, a software company that helps companies automate invoice processing.

The digital signals generated by almost every activity in our increasingly connected world, combined with cheap and plentiful storage and computing power to sift through them, comprise what's now known as big data. It is a somewhat ill-defined concept, but Gartner, a consultancy, reckons that spending on the software and systems required to mine vast troves of data will reach $55 billion in 2016, double the investment in big data five years earlier.

It is a common assertion by government intelligence agencies that in order to find a needle in a haystack, you need a haystack. This is a similar principle to big data, in that organisations are no longer limited to selective sampling of data in looking for evidence to test a theory or support a decision; hoovering up all available information and testing for correlations gets the job done with less scope for errors and omissions.

Or so the theory goes. The lure of near-unlimited information to inform decision-making is powerful, but CFOs must beware of drowning their organisations in data, blindly following spurious correlations, or blunting a company's creative drive. In their book *Big Data*, Viktor Mayer-Schönberger and Kenneth Cukier warn of a slavish devotion to "black boxes that offer us no accountability, traceability, or confidence". What is needed, they argue, is a new corporate role, the "algorithmist", who vets big data predictions. They describe these managers in a way that is familiar to financial executives:

They could take two forms – independent entities to monitor firms from outside, and employees or departments to monitor them from within – just as companies have in-house accountants as well as outside auditors who review their finances.

In addition to the extra layers of governance necessary to steer big data initiatives, the mountain of information now collected by companies also creates new risks that need addressing. With information increasingly stored in the "cloud" instead of on internal, offline systems, the opportunity for breaches and leaks of potentially sensitive data is heightened. Securities regulators require increasingly detailed disclosures following successful cyber-attacks, with reports on a company's preventative measures a likely focus for future reporting requirements. Despite big data's promise to help companies make better-informed decisions, CFOs need to make sure that none of the information companies now collect falls into the wrong hands.

Investors

Looking outside the company, one of the most important external relationships for many CFOs is with investors. On average, CFOs at listed companies spend around a day a week on investor relations. Around quarter- and year-ends, however, the rounds of investor and analyst meetings can be all-consuming. Every shareholder or analyst has different motivations and demands an audience with the finance chief. As in so many other contexts, the CFO is expected to provide an unvarnished, clear-eyed assessment of company performance in the past, present and future. Bruce Besanko, CFO of SuperValu, a Minnesota-based retailer, explained the process in a report published by Ernst & Young:

> I have found that most investors like to spend about 20% of their time with a CEO, 60% of their time with the CFO, and another 20% of their time with other business unit leaders in the company. And the reason for that is they get more of the numbers story for their models from the CFO.

Even so, few CFOs believe that the models investors use to value their companies are entirely accurate. Naturally, most finance chiefs think that their companies' shares are undervalued.[2] And although they would never disparage the owners of their companies publicly, off the record one dismisses the City of London as "like a school playground" while another describes brokerage analysts as "teenage scribblers", a slur coined by Nigel Lawson, a former UK chancellor of the exchequer, to deride economic analysts critical of his policies. Greater turnover in company shares – as reflected in shorter average holding times (see Figure 4.1) – means that relationships with investors are much less durable than in the past.

Although explaining a company's financial performance over and over again to a rotating cast of investors can be a chore, it is the best way to ensure that a company's valuation best reflects its prospects. And many, if not most, CFOs say that meeting with investors and analysts gives them a better feel for how their companies are perceived, which directs their focus to areas where they can make the most impact.

FIG 4.1 **Average holding period for shares**
Years

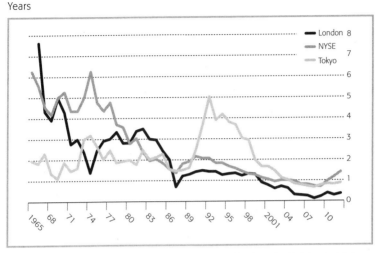

Sources: London Stock Exchange; New York Stock Exchange (NYSE); Tokyo Stock Exchange

Given their stature, investors pay close attention to what CFOs say, so any slip-up while fielding questions or giving presentations of company results can potentially trigger turbulence in a company's shares. Securities regulators impose strict rules governing the release of company information to the markets, so caution generally reigns when it comes to investor relations. Still, CFOs need to be honest and reliable when they speak with investors, even when times are tough, as Robin Freestone, CFO of Pearson, a UK publishing company (and part owner of *The Economist*), explained in *Real Business* magazine:

> *Shareholders and stakeholders are not stupid. They work in complex organisations which are far from perfect and they know that all companies have issues. Denial is not a credible position; implying perfection merely attracts suspicion. Far better to explain where things are not going well, and what you're attempting to do to put them right. That approach is so rare that investors will sit up and listen.*

Investors inevitably want more information about a company's past performance and future plans than a CFO can conceivably share. But studies show that companies often benefit from investor communications with richer information about key business drivers and related non-financial data that go beyond what they are legally required to publish.

In one fascinating example, Coloplast, a Danish health-care products company, produced two versions of a report detailing its latest annual performance. One included a welter of non-financial data related to its operational performance, detailing the company's strategic goals and explaining its economic context. The other stripped out these voluntary data points, leaving only the narrative and financial accounts required by regulators.

Two sets of analysts at a British asset-management firm were given the reports and asked to come up with financial forecasts, a recommendation to buy or sell the stock, and an estimate of how risky future returns would be compared with the company's rivals. The analysts with just the financial information came up with higher average forecasts, but most judged the shares too risky and recommended that they be sold. The group with more complete reports came up with lower forecasts but were bullish on the company's shares; their earnings estimates were also within a much narrower range than those of the group with just the financial information.

If sharing more information with investors improves the perception of company performance, what holds companies back? The tortured debate over how – or even whether – to provide guidance to the markets on earnings, revenue or other financial measures is relevant in this regard. Of US-listed companies surveyed by the National Investor Relations Institute in late 2012, 75% said that they provided public financial guidance, compared with 85% three years earlier.

Sharing targets with investors and analysts is good for focusing them on performance that the company thinks is achievable. But it can be a dangerous game. Judy Brown, CFO of Perrigo, a US health-care company, told the *Wall Street Journal*:

> If you build expectations, then you have to live by those expectations. That's an art because you are looking into a crystal

ball, whereas closing the books is a science. So you are trying to marry an art and science.

For CFOs, the penalties for missing analysts' forecasts – the so-called consensus estimate for earnings – are severe. Falling short of the market's expectations can result in a pay cut or even a sacking. This is because of many boards' fixation on staying in the market's good graces, punishing a small miss of the consensus number much more severely than rewarding a minor beat. This can tempt finance chiefs to "manage" earnings in unhelpful – or illegal – ways, and more generally complicates their goal of driving performance in both the short and long term.

The global financial crisis in 2008 was useful, in a way, because it exposed the folly of financial forecasts during uncertain times. Many companies suspended quarterly guidance during the depths of the crisis and refused to revive the practice when conditions improved. Longer-term guidance, often featuring a range of expected outcomes a year or more into the future, steers the markets in a company's preferred direction without encouraging them to fixate on a discrete, short-term target.

Investor relations was not always such a fraught discipline. In a 1964 book based on a survey of financial executives in the United States, LeBaron Foster reached a rather striking conclusion:

> *Of all the principal public groups having a stake in the corporation's progress, investors appear the least complaining and the least demanding. Management finds few fires to extinguish, and rarely hears serious rumblings of revolt.*

These days, a company's shares are frequently set alight by high-frequency trading, comprising powerful computers trading in huge volumes every second based on complex algorithms that are wholly uninterested in the firm's long-term financial performance. These machines, which thrive on volatility, account for around 50% of equity trades in the United States and 40% in Europe, according to Tabb Group, a research firm.

CFOs are also almost constantly fighting fires when dealing with investors, whether it is fielding thorny questions about earnings guidance or, increasingly, fending off uppity "activist" investors who buy stakes in a company in order to agitate for significant changes in strategy. Activist hedge funds seek out companies they believe are undervalued or incompetent and harangue management to change course, often pushing – noisily and publicly – for share buy-backs, bigger dividends or divestments that they believe would reward shareholders more richly. Activists are taking on larger companies than they used to, and signs suggest that traditionally sedate investors, such as pension funds, are more amenable to their methods, lending support to their crusades in a growing number of cases.

The proliferation of social-media channels adds another tricky dimension to investor relations, as Julie Eastland, CFO of Oncothyreon, a NASDAQ-listed biotechnology company, explains:

> Drug trials go on for years, and we have not had a lot to say that is different over those years. But people can put their views on some sites and they will appear alongside company press releases. There is a lot of credibility given to these opinions and it can create big shocks.

The shocks can also come from the inside. In May 2012, Gene Morphis was dismissed as CFO of Francesca's Holdings, a US-listed retailer, after he tweeted about board meetings on his personal account. One of his tweets – "Board meeting. Good numbers=Happy Board" – could be construed as market-sensitive information, which is required to be released publicly via official corporate channels.

This mistake by an otherwise compliance-minded CFO shows how treacherous financial communications have become in modern times. Some 85% of class-action securities lawsuits in the United States cite "materially false and misleading statements" as the cause, which means that CFOs must always be on their toes when sharing information with the investment community.

Privately held firms may not be subject to the same heavy regulatory burden as publicly listed firms, but regardless of corporate structure CFOs are expected to provide company owners with the same robust, timely and reliable information. Private equity-owned companies, for example, may not need to publish quarterly reports

– or say much of anything about their performance publicly, for that matter – but in many ways the CFO's dealings with investors are every bit as intense, as described by Michael Clarke, finance director at ADAS, a private equity-owned company:

> *If you are moving in the direction that private equity wants you to move in, it doesn't matter that you don't deliver year-on-year growth, provided that you are taking steps towards the ultimate delivery of value.*

At the same time, the company's private equity owners require "huge amounts of detailed information", particularly operational and non-financial data:

> *It is certainly far more detailed information than you would ever provide to a listed company's board. I talk to my main shareholder every day.*

In the end, whether a company is private or public, family-owned or widely held, non-profit or for-profit, its owners will rely heavily on CFOs for information about the performance of their investments. John Rogers, president of the CFA Institute, an association that represents the investment industry, says:

> *Investors look to CFOs in order to feel confidence in the firm's stewardship. The ideal CFO is someone who has a degree of independence of judgment, and can express that in a certain way to investors, so that investors don't feel that they're being sold a line.*

Banks

For many companies, the global financial crisis in 2008 marked a turning point in the relationship between CFOs and bankers. The largest companies are usually able to access finance away from banks, but smaller firms rely heavily on bank loans to support investments and working capital. When this credit dried up thanks to the deepest downturn in a generation, already fragile relationships between finance chiefs and their companies' main banks frayed even further, if not severed entirely.

In a 2010 survey of US CFOs by *CFO* magazine, 25% of finance chiefs described the relationship with their company's primary bank as "strictly transactional", with another 20% calling it "deteriorating" or even "abysmal". Just over half of a group of finance executives surveyed in the UK in 2011 by *Financial Director* magazine said that the logistical difficulties in switching banks are what kept them with their current bank, which is hardly a ringing endorsement.

The retrenchment of big, global banks from many countries has opened the door for local or regional lenders – particularly in emerging markets – which gives CFOs new banking options. Finance chiefs are also generally more eager to shop around for banking services; for example, the share of global M&A advisory fees captured by "boutique" investment banks has grown from around 12% in 2003 to 20% in 2013, according to Thomson Reuters, a media and information company. Even if the so-called "bulge bracket" banks continue to capture the bulk of corporate banking business, CFOs can use the threat of a credible alternative to boost service levels or cut fees (or both).

When it comes to banking relationships, CFOs must balance the efficiencies that come from economies of scale – using one bank for a range of credit, advisory and transactional services – with the benefits of farming out a company's banking services across multiple providers. During the worst of the financial crisis, CFOs scrambled to diversify banking relationships, lest corporate cash get trapped in a failing bank. Patrick de La Chevardière, CFO of Total, a French oil company, explained the approach at his company to the *Wall Street Journal*:

> Total routinely works with 50 banks, and has been monitoring their health by keeping tabs on their debt ratings, the prices of their credit default swaps, and the sizes of their balance sheets, de La Chevardière said. He declined to provide specific levels at which the company triggers a change, but said that Total has shifted funds out of banks many times based on fluctuations in those metrics.
>
> "In 2011 it happened every day," he said. That was when fear of a collapse of the euro zone and consequently trouble for the region's banks was at its highest. "There were rumours everywhere," he said.

Total also happens to own a bank, and thus a banking licence, which gives it the option of parking cash at the national central bank, the ultimate safe haven. Other big companies, like most major auto companies, channelled funds via their financial services arms to central banks to their keep cash safe in a similar way.

Although improving economic conditions have made CFOs more comfortable trimming the number of banks that they work with, the lessons learned from the collapse of Lehman Brothers and the scare over a break-up of the euro zone are not quickly forgotten. More companies than ever are raising finance via the capital markets or non-bank credit providers – insurers, hedge funds, sovereign wealth funds and peer-to-peer lenders, to name a few. The travails of small suppliers in getting loans has also led some CFOs to extend credit from their companies' own resources, or to provide guarantees to the suppliers' banks on their behalf.

The tendency for banks to overcomplicate things – the fiendishly complex securities banks assembled using subprime mortgages exacerbated the financial crisis – is something else that CFOs guard against, now more than ever. Shortly after taking over as CFO at Essilor in 2007, Laurent Vacherot puzzled over a financial vehicle in which the company had invested a sizeable sum:

> The people inside Essilor, in the treasury department, said it was okay for this and that reason. The bankers said there was no problem with it. But the more questions I asked, the less I understood what was happening. We took the money out and put it elsewhere. Sometimes, you need to go back to basics. If you don't understand it, or can't understand it, there is something wrong.

Auditors

The churn in banking relationships, however modest, is positively frenetic compared with the turnover in a company's audit firm. The "Big Four" of Deloitte, Ernst & Young, KPMG and PricewaterhouseCoopers act as auditors for nearly every company of size, including all but two of the S&P 500. The tenure of a typical audit engagement often spans several decades, with only 2% of the UK's 350 largest listed firms switching auditors in any year. Deloitte has been Procter & Gamble's auditor since 1890.

Despite appearances, the relationship between companies and their audit firms is not as clubby as it once was, with the routine checks and approvals of a company's financial statements passing without much fuss. In 2002, the demise of Arthur Andersen, which shouldered some of the blame for the accounting scandal at Enron, put the rest of the audit world on notice. Avoiding similar charges means auditors are much more fastidious – some would say adversarial – about their work.

Regulators around the world are pushing for auditors to go beyond their usual boilerplate approval letters and publish detailed reports of their audit work alongside a company's accounts. To ensure their independence, many countries are investigating mandatory audit-firm rotation – or at least mandatory retendering of audit work – after a set number of years. Institutional investors also take an increasingly dim view of long audit tenures, fearing complacency or a loss of independence. Together, these factors make the CFO-auditor relationship much less cosy.

For regulators and shareholders, a beefed-up audit is a welcome layer of scrutiny on a company's accounting policies and procedures. For the CFO, it can be a disruptive annoyance, particularly if it takes the form of legalistic box-ticking instead of a genuine interrogation of internal controls and accounting practices. In a 2013 survey by *Financial Director* magazine, CFOs cited efficiency as the most important measure of an auditor's performance. One anonymous finance chief grumbled to the magazine that auditors are "an unnecessary evil and are a parasitic influence on innovation."

However strained relations have become with auditors, this is an extreme view. Even if audits have become an onerous ritual, they are also less costly. An investigation of the audit market by the UK government found that large listed firms cut the average inflation-adjusted audit fee per hour by 19% in the five years to 2011, while trimming the average hours per audit by 4% to boot. Jean Stephens, CEO of RSM International, a global accounting firm, says:

> Since the beginning of the global financial crisis, CFOs have had a razor sharp focus on cost cutting and this has extended to audit, which is becoming commoditised.

Audit firms accept lower fees for "commoditised" work because they often make it up via consulting services such as tax advice or strategic reviews. This presents another challenge for CFOs, who appreciate the audit firm's knowledge of the inner workings of their company but fear the perceptions of a conflict of interest in awarding audit and advisory work to the same firm. When RSA, an insurance company, planned to give extra consulting work to Deloitte – which it already paid more for consulting than for audit – some investors expressed unease. The company switched its auditor to KPMG in 2013.

Despite the criticisms about tenure and conflicts of interest, the Big Four's grip on the audit market does not appear in immediate jeopardy. CFOs argue that the size and scope of these firms makes them the only choices to audit complex, global operations. Even smaller, domestically focused firms cite some variation of this argument, which suggests that a simple herd instinct is the main driver. Although CFOs are increasingly keen to shop around with banks, their conservative nature comes to the fore with auditors.

Other vendors and service providers

As the keeper of the corporate chequebook, CFOs get pitched a wide variety of products and services. Whether it's a big-ticket IT system or a consulting engagement, vendors can expect heavy scrutiny.

Price is important, of course, but pitches that focus solely on cost will not pass muster. When asked to rank 12 factors in selecting a service provider in a 2011 survey by Martin Akel & Associates, a research firm, a group of CFOs said that the initial purchase price ranked tenth. It seems that many CFOs subscribe to the claim by a British tycoon, Sir James Goldsmith: "If you pay peanuts, you get monkeys." The vendor's attention to a company's specific needs ranked top in the survey, followed by the price-to-value relationship and a vendor's track record of reliability.

Chris Power is an experienced CFO of banks, securities and trading firms, including ABN Amro and CLS, from London to Hong Kong, Thailand and Brazil. At these heavily regulated firms that routinely oversee billions, if not trillions, of dollars in daily transactions, it is important to vet all purchases and partners carefully. Power describes what he looks for in a vendor:

> Clarity is the most important point for me, especially when it involves large and complex systems. At times, people deliberately create an opaque situation. We need to trust a supplier, because we will work with them for the long run. By being vague or unclear, that creates more doubts than anything to do with price. Even if you are up against, say, five other groups who appear to be cheaper but aren't so clear, you just cannot fully trust them. What is going to come out of the woodwork later?

This seems sensible, but Power reports a "mixed set" of approaches from vendors who have pitched to him over the years.

Even after a purchase is made, Power and other CFOs also stress the importance of maintaining a relationship with suppliers, keeping lines of communication open. "CFOs are characterised by an honest, open, direct style and they expect that to be reciprocated," according to Jonathan Jones, a director at BIE, a London-based financial recruitment firm. He adds:

> Far better, in my experience, to approach the CFO with a "heads up" to a problem than for them to be surprised by one self-discovered. If suppliers fail to deliver an agreed action plan, they can expect a very short relationship.

5   Prospects: a world of possibilities

WHAT DOES THE FUTURE hold for the role of the CFO? The characteristics of current CFOs, and the routes they took to the top finance post, offer some clues. After all, the type of CFO sought by a company reflects its future priorities. CFOs themselves are also more forthcoming about their own career ambitions, not least because the media and investors now take great interest in their aspirations, given how integral they are to a company's success.

According to Ernst & Young, more than 60% of CFOs at the world's largest companies in 2002 were still CFOs in 2012 or made finance chief their final executive role. Of the remainder, 15% went on to become CEO and the rest took up a variety of other roles. Today, the options available to CFOs – a function of their prominence, ever-expanding remits and the push for financial savvy in all corners of a company – make it likely that more of the finance chiefs in place in 2014 will have moved to different roles ten years down the line.

Where CFOs come from

Just over half of CFOs at large US firms were promoted internally, according to Crist/Kolder Associates. Two-thirds of these finance chiefs stepped up from controller, treasurer or divisional finance roles. There is much less variety in the source of externally appointed CFOs; more than half of them were CFOs at their previous firm.

Even though most CFOs are promoted from a financial role, their career up to that point is typically quite varied. McKinsey studied the career paths of CFOs at large companies hired before and after 2009 to see whether companies changed tack following the global financial crisis that began the year before. The more recent the hire, the more likely that the CFO spent some time outside finance and worked internationally, with around 60% of post-2009 CFO appointments boasting this globally minded, generalist background.

The vetting of potential CFOs is now much more sophisticated, according to Wolfgang Schmidt-Soelch of Korn/Ferry:

> *When I first joined recruiting seven years ago, there were CFO searches where the company said they just wanted a finance person who had a degree, speaks a certain language and had experience with SAP systems. It was experiential.*

Now, an intense battery of interviews, role-playing exercises, online assessments and psychometric tests try to measure a candidate's fit with the company's ideal profile. More time is spent sussing a candidate's leadership qualities, with lots of interview questions about past experience managing teams. In this vein, companies look to fill the CFO post with someone who complements the skills of other senior finance staff, instead of always going for an all-rounder. Suzzane Wood of Russell Reynolds says CFO searches often start with a SWOT analysis (strengths, weaknesses, opportunities and threats) of the company's finance team as a whole:

> *If they don't have a strong treasurer and there is a refinancing coming up, you can't really place a CFO learning that aspect on the job. But if they have a great treasurer, it won't be such a critical component of the brief.*

Jan Siegmund's appointment as CFO of ADP in late 2012 is a good example of how companies are thinking more expansively about what they want in a finance chief. A German working in the United States, Siegmund spent most of his career outside finance, as a consultant at McKinsey and in a variety of strategy and general management roles at ADP. He explains that the make-up of ADP's finance team and the company's unique circumstance at the time of his appointment also played a role:

> *The option for a non-conventional, strategic thinker as CFO offered itself because our company was in a great position. The board*

would not have made its decision if there was a lot of reconstruction
work to be done. This is not a save-the-company turnaround
situation, where different expertise might be needed. We have a deep
bench of functional experts in the finance team.

ADP is one of only four companies in the United States with a AAA
credit rating, so it has a uniquely strong balance sheet to manage. That
its CFO comes from such a non-traditional background shows that
all sorts of companies are thinking outside the box when it comes to
assessing CFO talent. According to Korn/Ferry, in the first half of 2013
a quarter of the CFOs appointed at the largest 1,000 companies in
the United States moved from a non-finance role; only 14% of CFOs
appointed in 2012 made the same move.

The more traditional route to CFO, of course, still applies. The
systematic development path mapped out at companies like GE,
PepsiCo, BP and others (discussed in detail in Chapter 3) hones
financial talent in a way that few other firms can, using functional and
geographic rotations to produce well-rounded financial managers. In
nearly 20 years at food giant Cadbury, "each time I needed a new
challenge they would come up with something that brought me into
a new facet of finance," says Alan Williams, now CFO of Greencore.

Becoming a finance chief is like joining an exclusive club, according
to the CFO of a medium-sized company listed in London:

A lot of boards will only take someone who has done the job. To get
a board to appoint a finance director who has not previously done
the role is quite a challenge. It's almost better to get into the club, no
matter what, than not get into the club.

This is what motivated the then financial controller to join a deeply
indebted firm a few years ago, even as it flirted with bankruptcy:

The company was in deep enough trouble that if it succeeded I
would have been a hero, but if it didn't it was always going to
happen and there was nothing you could do about it.

The scale of this challenge scared off many others, which gave him
the opportunity to take on his first top finance role at a listed firm. In
the end the company could not be saved, but his efforts impressed

the banks and advisers working to rescue the firm, which led in short order to his appointment as CFO at a bigger, healthier firm.

Qualified for the job

What makes a person qualified to be CFO? Given the responsibility for a company's accounts, it follows that most finance chiefs probably have an accounting qualification.

Not exactly. Only around a third of finance chiefs at the world's largest companies are chartered accountants. At these firms, more CFOs, around 40%, have MBA degrees.

This masks large regional variations. The UK remains a bastion of chartered accountants, with more than 80% of finance chiefs at FTSE 100 firms boasting this qualification. Similarly high percentages are seen in Australia and Singapore. Certified accountants are more rare in continental Europe and the United States. At Fortune 500 companies in the United States, around half of CFOs have an MBA degree, compared with 40% who are qualified accountants. Economics degrees, and more than a few PhDs, are relatively common in continental Europe.

Given the mix of financial acumen and general business skills required to succeed as a CFO these days, the qualifications of the average finance chief can be increasingly described as "all of the above". Around 10% of CFOs at large global companies are chartered accountants with MBA degrees.

Philip Symes is one of them. After studying mathematics at university, he qualified as an accountant during his early career at a forerunner of PricewaterhouseCoopers. He later added an MBA from London Business School. "I did an MBA to broaden out," as he explains:

> I'm part of a management team and I want to contribute on everything, not just finance. Some problems are not finance problems. Quite often, it's an organisational-design problem. My view of how an organisation works is far richer because I did an MBA. A lot of what I do is judgment, and that judgment needs to be in the context of the business as well as the financial aspects.

FIG 5.1 **Annual executive turnover at leading US companies**[a]
%

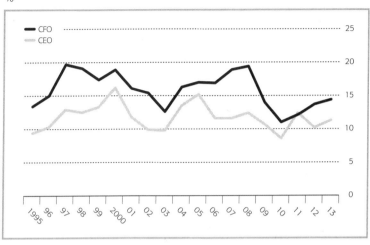

a *Fortune* 500 and S&P 500 firms (668 total in 2013).
Source: Crist/Kolder Associates

Value judgments

There are important regional wrinkles in the CFO job market, most notably that finance chiefs in Asia are overwhelmingly promoted from within, and many – if not most – spend their entire careers with the same company. To simplify greatly, the trends elsewhere are roughly similar to those in the United States, where companies change CFOs more often than CEOs (see Figure 5.1) and externally sourced CFOs are more common than CEOs plucked from the outside (see Figure 5.2).

Where the United States stands out is in the generosity of its pay packages.[1] In 2012, the median total compensation for CFOs at S&P 500 companies was worth more than $3m. The highest paid finance chief, Apple's Peter Oppenheimer, took home just under $70m, thanks mostly to share awards. At medium-sized companies with revenues of up to $1 billion, the CFO typically makes "only" around $1m per year.

At FTSE 100 companies in the UK, finance chiefs made around $2.5m, on average. Pay elsewhere in Europe, and in the rest of the world, tends to be more modest than in the UK and United States. It

FIG 5.2 **Share of external executive appointments at leading US companies[a]**

%

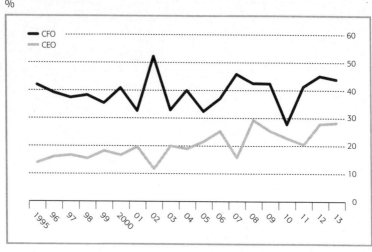

a *Fortune* 500 and S&P 500 firms (668 total in 2013).
Source: Crist/Kolder Associates

also typically features a larger fixed-salary component, whereas on average only around a quarter of pay packages for finance chiefs in the United States, the UK and at globally active listed firms comprise a cash salary, with bonuses, shares and other incentive-linked pay accounting for the rest.

In most countries, CEOs make two to three times more than the CFO, with bonus and share incentives comprising an even larger share of their overall pay package. In the United States, the top ten highest paid CEOs in 2012 all made more than $100m.

But in recent years, the demand for finance talent has pushed CFO salaries up faster than those of most other executive roles, including chief executive. Nearly 90% of CFOs at large US companies saw their salary rise in 2012, according to Compensation Advisory Partners, compared with only around 50% of CEOs. Looking at its placements between 2010 and 2012, Salveson Stetson, a recruitment firm, says CFOs earned an increase of 26% in compensation when changing jobs, well above the next-highest role, marketing, at 19%.

By now it is clear that the CFO role is, quite fittingly, financially rewarding. There is not too much time to get comfortable, though, as the typical tenure of a listed-company finance chief is now between four and six years, usually a year or so less than the average CEO's time in office. Internally appointed executives almost always serve for longer than externally appointed ones, which holds for both CEOs and CFOs.

The average CFO in the S&P 500 is around 52 years old, while finance chiefs in Europe tend to be a bit younger, in their late 40s. In most countries, the average age of executives has gradually fallen as managers are appointed to top posts earlier than in the past.

The gender gap

Despite steady, if slow, progress, women now hold around 10% of the CFO positions at S&P 500 and FTSE 100 companies. This may not sound like much, but it is still two to three times higher than the number of female CEOs at companies in the same sample.

FIG 5.3 **Share of female CFOs at large listed companies**[a]
%

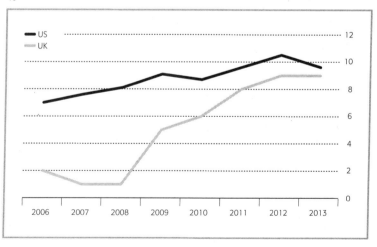

a FTSE 100 in the UK; Fortune 500 and S&P 500 in the United States.
Sources: Cranfield School of Management; Crist/Kolder Associates

The average female CFO is a bit younger and stays in the job for slightly less time than her average male counterpart. But GMI Ratings, a research firm, found that even after controlling for these and other company-specific factors, men earned 16% more than women in CFO roles at listed US firms.

This disparity is not because of a difference in responsibilities. In fact, research by Equilar, a data provider, found that some 60% of female finance chiefs in the S&P 500 held an outside board seat as a non-executive director in addition to their CFO responsibilities. Only 22% of male CFOs could say the same.

New horizons

To address their finance chiefs' ambitions, and keep them interested in the role, companies are charging CFOs with a host of new responsibilities on top of their traditional duties. This can take the form of official responsibility for running a business unit or customer segment. In a global survey of more than 4,000 CFOs in 2012 by Michael Page International, 51% said that they expected to stay in their current role for the next two years, but with a bigger scope; this was three times the number who expected to stay put, content with the existing scope of their role.

In mid-2013, the backgrounds of CFOs at 200 leading global firms – the largest 50 listed companies in the Americas, Europe and Asia, and the 50 largest privately held firms – were researched for this book. Around 15% of finance chiefs at these firms carried formal responsibility for a business unit alongside their CFO role. Examples include regional divisions, product-focused units and high-level company-wide initiatives like sustainability. This is more prevalent in Europe than in other regions, and at non-financial corporations more than financial services firms.

Another option open to sitting CFOs is a non-executive directorship on an outside board. "The most noticeable change over the past decade is that the demand for CFOs on boards has increased dramatically," says Wood of Russell Reynolds. Nearly 50% of CFOs at the 350 largest global firms held a non-executive role in 2012, compared with 36% ten years earlier, according to Ernst & Young. Many countries now mandate that at least one financial expert – which many read to mean current or former CFO – sits on a company's board, which explains why 21% of S&P 500 boards featured a financial expert in 2003, while 100% do today. These days, it is increasingly rare for an audit committee chairman not to have CFO experience.

Sitting around the table in another company's boardroom, "there are issues you face that you haven't come across in your executive role," says Julian Metherell, CFO of Genel Energy and non-executive director at GasLog, a shipping company. "You never leave a board meeting without being challenged about how you think of your own business." This value is reflected in research that shows companies with CFOs who serve on outside boards generate a higher return for shareholders, according to research in 2013 by Equilar. These CFOs also earn more than their counterparts who do not hold non-executive positions, which is another sign of their worth to their employers.

This raises the question: where do CFOs find the time to do all this? Nick Aitchison of The Ashton Partnership, a recruitment firm, urges caution:

> I know several CFOs who chair the audit committee at other companies, which is a huge dual responsibility. If I was a CEO, I'd be delighted for my CFO to be on another board, but I don't think I'd want that person to be the audit chair, because of the extra responsibility. It gives the CFO two year-ends to deal with, and one is bad enough.

There have not been any time-and-motion studies of CFOs to determine how they fit all their work into the average day – much less the mental agility required to juggle so many tasks at once – but suffice to say that conversations with top finance chiefs rarely revolve around long holidays or elaborate weekend plans.

Eventually, finance chiefs cannot amass any more responsibilities without their core duties suffering. Then the time comes for a new challenge.

Money movers

The global financial crisis in 2008, and its attendant shockwaves, put a lot of bankers out of work. Even for those that survived the cull, the turbulence now endemic in the banking industry makes the supposedly more sedate, secure career as a CFO more appealing to high-flying banking rainmakers.

Recruiters report a rise in applications from former bankers setting their sights on CFO roles. But although both roles are superficially similar in many ways, making the transition is not easy. For fear of antagonising current and future clients, few headhunters are willing to speak about this on the record. This is how one recruiter describes a common misconception among this particular group of job seekers:

> Investment bankers who have sold to CFOs, treasurers and other executives all think they can be CFOs. They'll call me and say so. They are very smart, but it's presumptuous because they don't have the operational experience. They think that people in industry go home at 6pm, but my people have always worked the same hours as the Wall Street guys.

This is not to say that bankers don't make good CFOs. It depends to a large degree, however, on a company's circumstances, with those raising capital, making deals and facing other transaction-centric initiatives being best suited for finance chiefs with a banking background. Senior bankers who advise companies on deals are best placed to join them as CFOs, given their familiarity with the business and the board of directors' familiarity with them.

That is how Julian Metherell, a former partner at Goldman Sachs who specialised in the energy industry, made his way to upstream oil and gas group Genel Energy. A banking background "gives you a numeracy, literacy and a particular understanding of the financing part of the job," he says. The high-stakes negotiations that come with the consolidation of the energy industry make it a popular place for former bankers seeking corporate finance roles. Appraising investments and dealing with investors also come naturally to bankers, Metherell says.

Up and away

"Today I'm relatively indifferent whether I do a finance role or a commercial role," says Jim Buckle, CFO of Wiggle. "It's about finding interesting opportunities at interesting businesses." Many young accountants, auditors or controllers just starting out see CFO as the pinnacle of achievement on the corporate finance ladder. Wood of Russell Reynolds says:

> They go into their career thinking of it as a destination, but what happens is that there are more opportunities post that destination than there once were.

In most surveys, between a quarter and a third of CFOs say that they aspire to a position outside finance for their next move. Among this group, it should be no surprise that the most popular destination is CEO, particularly among younger finance chiefs and those in North America. This ambition is something Aitchison of The Ashton Partnership sees when recruiting for CFO posts: "I've had CFO searches where for the person we wanted we were in competition not with other CFO roles but with CEO roles," he says. Another recruiter, Schmidt-Soelch of Korn/Ferry, notes that the ranks of future CEOs among the current crop of CFOs are probably larger than the surveys suggest:

> CFO candidates still view the step up to CEO as less of an option than other business leaders. They are probably more humble and realistic in their expectations. Regional or divisional heads would automatically aim for the top job. CFOs are absolutely aware that they are probably viewed as a successor – in fact, they are in a better position than some other leaders.

This describes Denise Ramos at ITT. As CFO of the conglomerate since 2007, the chief executive post "was not in my sights, to be honest with you," she recalls. But when the subject was broached in 2011, "it sounded intriguing," she says. "To some degree, I had been thinking like that my entire career. CFOs need to understand that they should always think like a CEO."

Ramos remains rare in the sense that direct promotions from

FIG 5.4 **Financial background of CEOs appointed at leading US companies**[a]
%

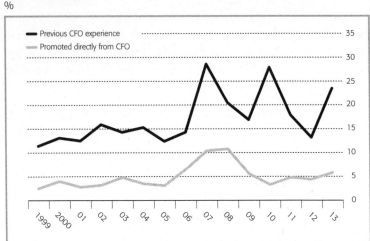

a *Fortune* 500 and S&P 500 firms (668 total in 2013).
Source: Crist/Kolder Associates

CFO to CEO are not too common. That said, the share of CEOs with finance experience is sizeable; around a quarter of chief executives appointed in 2013 at the United States's largest listed firms were once CFOs (see Figure 5.4). Around half of chief executives appointed in 2012 and 2013 in the UK's FTSE 100 have a finance background, with 12% promoted directly from CFO, according to Robert Half.

Thus for CFOs with designs on the top spot, the usual pattern is to prove oneself as a general manager by moving into a role as divisional president or head of a business before making the leap to CEO. Telefónica appears to subscribe to this theory, packing its executive committee with financial talent. In late 2013, in addition to its serving CFO, three of the nine-person committee were former CFOs (of the group or an important business unit) running regional and product divisions.

After seven years as CFO of SSAB, a Swedish steel company, Martin Lindqvist was offered the chance to run one of the firm's product units in 2008. He was soon promoted to head of the group's largest regional divisions and, within three years of stepping out of the finance department, was named CEO of the company. For other finance executives considering a move into general management, Lindqvist has simple advice: "If you get the opportunity, take it." Shortly after he took on his first executive role outside the finance function, he says he realised that he could have done this earlier.

Although all types of companies see the benefits of financial experience in executive appointments, some are keener on promoting CFOs than others. Mature, heavily regulated industries like energy, financial services and telecoms are more likely to install a former finance chief at the helm than are retailers or fast-growing technology firms.

Regardless of industry, a company's economic circumstances also influence its preference in a CEO. Companies undertaking big restructuring projects or with similar heavy financial commitments are more inclined to promote a CFO to the top job. For example, Marcel Smits was promoted from finance chief to CEO at Sara Lee, a US consumer products company, in 2011. In a year as chief executive he rationalised the company's product portfolio and, ultimately, oversaw a split of the company in two: US-based food group Hillshire Brands and Netherlands-based coffee and tea business DE Master Blenders 1753. Around the same time, Ian Dyson led a similar demerger as CEO of Punch Taverns, a UK pub operator, which he joined as CEO after a stint as finance chief at retailer Marks & Spencer. While CFO at ITT, Ramos helped develop a plan to spin off the group's water and defence businesses. When the "new" ITT was unveiled following the divestments – now focused on the energy, transport and industrial markets – she was tapped as CEO.

Despite the increasingly wide range of activities that CFOs are charged with managing, stepping up to CEO remains a daunting challenge. The switch from an adviser and influencer on strategy to the ultimate decision-maker on these matters is a significant one. Many CFOs who become CEOs say that they spend a disproportionate amount of time travelling, meeting as many people across a company's operations as possible. The old stereotype of the CFO dies hard, so in face-to-face conversations and small group meetings, former finance chiefs can explain the breadth of the modern CFO role, especially its operational and strategic aspects, to the rank and file who might be sceptical of a CEO who rose via the finance function.

And although financial nous is clearly an advantage that former CFOs bring to the CEO's office, relying too heavily on it can be risky. This is how Michael Ward, a former CFO who was tapped to run Harrods, a luxury department store, in 2005, put it to a reporter from *Accountancy* magazine:

> *It's best if you leave quite a lot of your training behind – otherwise you become overanalytical. We're close to the figures here, we follow them very carefully. But this is a business about taste and style, it relies on the natural instinct of the merchants. It's quite difficult to work that into analytical models.*

Another challenge for CFOs that step up to CEO is forging a good relationship with the person who takes over as finance chief. "I walk the line very carefully," says Ramos of ITT:

> *There is good and bad. The good is that he doesn't have to explain a lot to me. The negative part is that I know a lot about the job, and there are certain things I can probe and press on that another CEO wouldn't. You need to be careful to utilise those things in a productive way. It's his job, it's not my job.*

Thinking ahead

Milton Friedman, an economist, said: "The social responsibility of business is to increase its profits." On its face, this sentiment seems aimed squarely at CFOs. But finance chiefs increasingly subscribe to a much broader definition of corporate performance, incorporating environmental, social and other measures of "sustainability" alongside financial results.

In part, this is due to a growing public awareness of sustainability issues. According to Jean-Marc Huët, CFO of Unilever:

> *Our customers and the people who use our products are starting to care more about these issues and they are starting to vote with their wallets.*

The CEO of Unilever, former Nestlé CFO Paul Polman, has made sustainability a key focus for the company, incorporating new, long-term environmental and social measures into its reports while scrapping short-term practices like quarterly financial reports and earnings guidance. Huët and the company's finance department are the stewards of sustainability information, as he explains:

> My team has been working to first ensure that the metrics are fit for purpose and are sufficiently robust to integrate into our regular performance reporting. The next step is to embed these metrics into the scorecards which our senior leaders use to drive progress.

The growing involvement of CFOs in measuring and managing sustainability is not a coincidence. In a 2012 survey of corporate executives by Ernst & Young, respondents said that the biggest driver of the "sustainability agenda" is cost reduction. In addition to lowering costs by cutting waste or using fewer raw materials, companies with strong sustainability credentials also often find favour in the markets, with a lower cost of debt and equity capital. The increasing importance of social and environmental criteria in the investment plans of large asset managers is further motivation for CFOs to embrace sustainability.

At Interserve, a UK-listed construction and support services group, Tim Haywood's official title is Group Finance Director and Head of Sustainability. "Sustainable business is good business," he says. Reducing waste and resource consumption boosts efficiency, while fostering education and employment in local communities reduces worker turnover, increases productivity and bolsters the company's brand in the places where it operates. "As the finance director, I can see the financial implications of that," he adds.

In March 2013 Interserve launched an initiative called SustainAbilities, which details the 15 goals and 48 targets that the firm intends to meet or beat by 2020, covering everything from apprenticeships to employee health measures, energy and water use, and much else besides. Haywood dubs these "big hairy audacious goals" and says he spends around 20% of his time on sustainability matters. He adds:

> If I, as the company's chief sceptic, see that this makes sense, it makes it easier for everyone else in the organisation to appreciate the business case.

Branching out

At one time, CFOs approaching retirement age looked forward to a pension topped up by a few low-intensity non-executive directorships, working for only a few days a month. But the demand for finance chiefs on boards these days is so strong that CFOs are given directorships much earlier in their careers, often within a year or two of assuming the CFO role. This gives them more "runway" to aim for chairman roles, says Wood of Russell Reynolds. In some ways, she adds, CFOs are better suited to jump directly to chairman instead of chief executive roles anyway:

> In a chairman role, you look for somebody who's prudent with a low ego, good judgment and is a facilitator. The low-ego, second-in-command nature of a CFO sits very well for the non-executive chairman brief. We've had CFOs in their early 50s make the move into chairmanship.

There are much fewer examples of CFO-to-chairman moves than CFO-to-CEO moves, but this seems likely to change in the near future. When Andrew Higginson, a long-time finance chief of Tesco, a retailer, left the group in 2012 he took on two chairmanships, at N Brown, a listed fashion group, and Poundland, a private equity-owned retailer. "[Finance directors] make quite good chairmen, better than chief executives," Higginson told *Financial Director* magazine. Of his full-time move into the boardroom(s), he said:

> The alternative was to get a chief executive job elsewhere, but it would be hard to get the same buzz. At 55, I still wanted to be reasonably hands on and a chairmanship keeps me involved.

There are plenty of other "hands on" options for finance chiefs looking beyond the traditional CFO, CEO and director roles. After Chris Liddell spent eight years as CFO at International Paper, Microsoft and General Motors, he stepped off the traditional corporate ladder in 2011 and used his financial management skills in Mitt Romney's 2012 US presidential campaign. In mid-2013, at age 53, he told CFO magazine, "It's very unlikely that you'll see me in a traditional CFO role again." He explained why:

Been there, done that. I've had three fantastic ones in a row, and I enjoyed each of them and they were enormously satisfying ... I'm more interested in variety and new challenges than going back and doing the same thing again.

The versatility of a CFO's skillset and the growing demand for their expertise in a wide range of contexts are indeed opening a new spectrum of options for finance chiefs looking for "variety and new challenges". State-owned companies and sovereign wealth funds in emerging markets are hoovering up financial talent from the West as they grow in stature and expand globally. The non-profit sector has also seen an influx of former private-sector CFOs applying their know-how to charitable organisations that are increasingly adopting more commercial approaches to managing their resources and delivering services.

Private equity firms are also keen on hiring finance chiefs, both to help their funds vet potential investments and to parachute them into portfolio companies on short-term assignments. They are charged with revamping a company quickly so that the fund can realise its investment within a few years of buying it. Private equity firms are essentially in the business of financial engineering, so CFOs of portfolio companies owned by these funds are given free rein to operate with few reporting requirements and an equity stake that pays off handsomely if they are able to boost a company's fortunes and pass it on to an acquirer or list it on the stockmarket.

In a similar vein, another growing industry is interim finance placements and project-based consulting. David Bloom spent 20 years in finance at listed firms in the technology and media sectors before setting up FDU, a London-based agency that places finance chiefs at fast-growing firms for short assignments. He says:

These companies need someone with energy who can roll their sleeves up and get stuck in. With the standardisation of systems and processes, it's very easy for good CFOs to migrate from one company to another and provide added value almost on day one.

Other "serial CFOs" use listed-company expertise to help companies in the transition from a private to public company. Steve

Cakebread spent a bit more than two years at Pandora, an online music company, doing just that, and the company paid him nearly $1.8m – three times the CEO's compensation – in 2011, the year he helped take the firm public. In 2012 Doug Fenstermaker, a veteran CFO of hospital systems across the United States, joined Warbird Consulting Partners, a firm that places former finance chiefs like him on short-term projects for overburdened CFOs at health groups like the ones he used to work for. Fenstermaker says:

> CFOs need clones of themselves to get things done. We bring in people with 25–30 years' experience to help incumbent CFOs with a project or two.

But why choose just one thing? Seamus Keating is doing a bit of everything discussed above. After 24 years rising through the ranks in the technology sector, which included eight years as CFO and two as a regional business unit head at Logica, he shifted to a new phase in his career in 2012, just ahead of his 50th birthday. He has taken on a handful of directorships, including chairman at a financial technology firm in Dublin and audit committee head at a hospital group in Abu Dhabi. In addition, he advises technology-focused private equity firms on potential investments and serves as a mentor for first-time CFOs via Merryck & Company, a London-based leadership and executive coaching firm. "Rather than just looking at the next three years, I'm thinking about what will keep me interested for the next 20 years," he says.

Profit for a purpose

Caroline Stockmann rose through the ranks at KPMG before setting out on a finance career that included divisional CFO posts at big companies like Unilever and Novartis across Europe and Asia. She now finds herself as group CFO of another large, global organisation: Save the Children International, a non-profit group that campaigns for children's rights. She says:

> People come to a point when they want to add more back to the world, and they will take a salary cut in order to do so. For a finance person to take a pay cut it must be pretty important.

Save the Children operates in 120 countries and takes in $1.6 billion in revenue from government, corporate and personal donations every year. The scale of the challenges and the pace of the job match anything she faced in the corporate world. "We aim for the same professional standards as at Unilever, but on a much smaller budget," she says. Her fellow executives boast equally impressive corporate credentials, coming from places like Procter & Gamble, Kimberly-Clark and Thomson Reuters. The organisation works with leading consultants, lawyers and other professional service firms, which donate their services pro bono to the group.

The responsibilities of a CFO at a non-profit company are similar to those at a for-profit one, with a few notable exceptions. Non-profits must spend nearly all of their income, so budgets and delivery plans need to be flexible in case a big grant or award comes in unexpectedly. Donors also increasingly specify that their money should go only towards programmes, which can leave an organisation scrambling for funds to cover the necessary infrastructure and overheads to deliver the programmes in the first place. The mission of an organisation like Save the Children also takes it to places most commercially minded companies avoid; co-ordinating more than 100 grants worth more than $100m in Ethiopia, for example, is a daunting challenge for Stockmann and her finance team.

Zarin Patel, who left the BBC in mid-2013 after serving as CFO for nine years, says the "sheer seductiveness of belonging to an organisation that everyone knows and loves" is what attracts a lot of financial talent to non-profit and public-service organisations, at all stages of their careers. In addition to contributing to an organisation's social mission, the intellectual challenges are rewarding. "If you don't have a bottom line you have to explain things in a different way," she says.

Although their training teaches CFOs to think in logical steps, it requires greater "emotional intelligence" to motivate and manage staff when profit is not an important measure, Patel says. Taking a cue from the broadcasters she worked with, she learned good storytelling skills, building a compelling narrative behind financial goals and targets. "In the public sector you have to think about the story," she says. "It's profit for a purpose."

Omniscient and omnipresent

As detailed throughout this book, the rise of the CFO is one of the defining traits of the evolution of the modern corporation. The responsibilities now heaped on finance executives – and the financial acumen firms demand from all employees, not just those in the finance department – are reshaping the way that companies work.

Finance managers are exposed to a wider range of activities earlier in their careers and, as a result, enjoy an influence that extends further than ever before. The upshot is that, for many, CFO is now a step on the career ladder instead of its apex. Bernardo Mingrone, appointed CFO of Italy's third-largest bank, Monte dei Paschi di Siena, a couple of years before turning 40, is clear about his career goals:

> My ultimate ambition is not being CFO of a large institution. I would like to be a CEO or a general manager. Having gained the commercial experience in investment banking – you are effectively a salesperson – I'm now completing the course of my career with technical skills like greater accounting knowledge, tax planning and treasury management.

The churn in top finance posts also means that it is increasingly common for managers who spend the bulk of their careers in corporate finance to pass a decade or more at the pinnacle of the profession by the time they turn 50. The impatient, results-oriented view of performance may push them from the CFO post at one company to another, but eventually many decide to apply their skills in a different setting. A growing number of finance managers, like Mingrone, have their sights on other positions from an early stage, with experience in finance serving as the route to get them there. Some companies treat the top finance post as one of many stops on the development path for high-potential executives, rotating them through the CFO office regardless of whether they have prior experience in the finance department.

Some fear that this raises the risk that the company's chief steward, blinded by ambition, will ignore the key fiduciary duties of the CFO role. Even worse, short tenures and skewed incentives may encourage the executive charged with maintaining internal controls and managing risks to cut corners in order to boost short-term performance (and thus their own career prospects). These worries are largely unfounded, for two reasons.

First, the CFO's stature and influence arise from the post's privileged access to information across a firm, making the finance chief a trusted adviser to boardroom colleagues and a crucial conduit providing information about company performance to external stakeholders. As the volume of data companies can collect to gauge this performance expands exponentially, it is the CFO who is charged with interpreting it, imbuing the role with an air of omniscience. In this data-driven context, missteps are punished severely and fall disproportionately on the CFO, who is assumed to have all the answers. If anything goes wrong on their watch, a CFO's ambitions will be swiftly curtailed.[2] Live by the numbers, die by the numbers.

Second, as more CFOs move into positions beyond finance, finance chiefs gain an ever-expanding group of allies. At many companies, the chances are that the CEO, directors and business-unit heads will all have spent time in the finance function at some point during their careers, if not in the CFO post itself. Their understanding of the tensions inherent in the role makes them aware of the challenges that CFOs face, as they themselves may have struggled to strike the balance between steward and strategist at one time. This makes them less likely to pressure CFOs to betray their principles or compromise their independence.

The image of the CFO as an isolated accountant toiling quietly in an insular function is obsolete. In a sense, the corporate world is now filled with CFOs, and not only in the finance department.

Notes and sources

Introduction
Note
1 Other descriptions of the role of the CFO collected by the author include: analyst, architect, activist, catalyst, challenger, champion, change agent, coach, collaborator, confidant, cop, co-pilot, critic, custodian, conscience, counterweight, dealmaker, diplomat, driver, facilitator, gatekeeper, guardian, influencer, integrator, mentor, myth buster, operator, pathfinder, pioneer, regulator, sorcerer, steward, strategist, sounding board, scorekeeper and translator. There are many, many more.

Source
Reuters, "Bank of America CFO de Molina resigning", December 1st 2006

1 Origins: from the back office to the front line
Notes
1 In a study of more than 400 of the largest companies in America, Dirk Zorn of Princeton University reckons that the first formal appointment of a "chief financial officer" was by Dan River Mills, a textile manufacturer, in February 1966, when it promoted its treasurer, C. Eugene Rowe, to the position.
2 The origins of modern accounting can be traced back much further, to the invention of double-entry book-keeping by Italian merchants in the 14th century. As early as the 15th century, the English royal household employed both a comptroller and

treasurer. These titles were in use in public administrations long before they became common in a corporate context.

3   A group of European professors tracked the shift in the image of finance executives around this time in a novel way: by analysing the advertisements aimed at financial managers in the pages of professional publications produced by the UK's Chartered Institute of Management Accountants. From the tone of the ads, the researchers observed that in the 1970s and 1980s, the finance executive was pitched as a "responsible and rational accountant, providing information for rational decisions". In the 1990s, by contrast, there emerged "a more adventurous and powerful image of accountants, as daring and thrill-seeking explorers". See Baldvinsdottir, G., Burns, J., Norreklit, H. and Scapens, R., "The image of accountants: from bean counters to extreme accountants", *Accounting, Auditing & Accountability Journal*, 2009.

4   Doing justice to these cases and related scandals requires a book of its own. That book is *Creative Accounting, Fraud and International Accounting Scandals* by Michael Jones (Wiley, 2010).

Sources

Anderson, M. and Gerstner Jr., L., "The chief financial officer as activist", *Harvard Business Review*, September-October 1976

Bateson, W., *Organization and Administration of the Finance Department*, Sir I. Pitman & Sons, 1924

Chandler Jr., A., *The Visible Hand: The Managerial Revolution in American Business*, Harvard University Press, 1977

Dierkes, J., Dobbin, F., Kwok, M. and Zorn, D., *Cui Bono: Institutional Investors, Securities Analysts, Agents, and the Shareholder Value Myth*, paper presented at the "New Public and Private Models of Management: Sensemaking and Institutions" conference at Copenhagen Business School, May 2005

The Economist, CFO Summit, London, January 2013

Fligstein, N., *The Transformation of Corporate Control*, Harvard University Press, 1990

Haase, P., *Financial Executives Institute: The First Forty Years*, Financial Executives Institute, 1971

ICAEW, *Finance in the broadest sense*, 2013

2 Role: ensuring control, driving strategy
Notes

1 It is worth noting that the benefits of improved financial
   reporting quality were offset, in part, by CFOs with board
   positions commanding higher pay and proving harder to dismiss
   following periods of poor performance.
2 See Francis, B., Shin, Y. and Wang, W., "Are CFOs' Trades
   More Informative Than CEOs' Trades?", *Journal of Financial
   and Quantitative Analysis*, August 2012; and Knewtson, H.,
   *CEOs, CFOs, and COOs: Why are Certain Insiders' Trades more
   Informative?*, April 2011.
3 Since "insiders" like CFOs and CEOs are required to report
   their trades publicly, efficient-market theory suggests that if
   CFOs' trading profits were the sole result of them reflexively
   manipulating earnings to suit their portfolios, other investors
   would quickly price this in and erode the outperformance.
4 At the risk of comparing apples and oranges, in 2006 Deutsche
   Bank surveyed more than 300 executives on the value provided
   by their finance departments. On average, respondents put the
   finance function's worth at just over 10% of a company's market
   capitalisation. In the context of a department that costs only
   around 1% of revenue to run, that is a pretty good return.

Sources

Accenture, Oracle and Longitude Research, *The CFO as Catalyst for
   Change*, May 2013
Achleitner, A., Lutz, E., and Schraml, S., *Loss of Control vs. Risk
   Reduction – Decision Factors for Hiring Non-Family CFOs in Family
   Firms*, CEFS Working Paper Series, July 2011
Barkin, N., "Ackermann Rejects Blame for 'Tragic' Wauthier Suicide",
   Reuters, September 12th 2013
Bedard, J., Hoitash, R. and Hoitash, U., "Chief Financial Officers as
   Inside Directors", *Contemporary Accounting Research*, forthcoming
Caselli, S. and Di Guili, A., "Does the CFO Matter in Family Firms?
   Evidence from Italy", *The European Journal of Finance*, 2010
Collins, D., Masli, A., Reitenga, A. and Sanchez, J., "Earnings

Restatements, the Sarbanes-Oxley Act, and the Disciplining of Chief Financial Officers", *Journal of Accounting, Auditing & Finance*, Winter 2009

Engelen, A. and Venus, A., *A Strategy Perspective on the Performance Relevance of the CFO*, Technical University Dortmund Discussion Paper, February 2012

Enrich, D. and Morse, A., "Friction at Zurich Built in Months Before Suicide", *Wall Street Journal*, September 4th 2013

Ernst & Young, *Views. Vision. Insights. The evolving role of today's CFO*, 2012

Hope, J., *Reinventing the CFO*, Harvard Business School Press, 2006

ICAEW, *Leadership: A Finance & Management Special Report*, December 2012

ICAEW, *The Finance Function: A Framework for Analysis*, September 2011

McCann, D., "Seeking CFOs with Vision – and More", CFO.com, June 3rd 2013

Michael Page International, *Global CFO Barometer 2012*, August 2012

Teach, E., "The Best Medicines", CFO, March 2013

3 Responsibilities: internal affairs
Notes

1 GE even managed to create an entirely new business from what was once its finance and accounting shared service centre. As the India-based operation took on work from a variety of functions, other companies took note of its contribution to GE's famed organisational processes. In 2005 it was spun off as an independent company and took on clients from outside GE. Now called Genpact, it employs more than 60,000 people and generates annual revenues of around $2 billion.

2 Accounting conservatism, broadly, can be measured via signs in financial statements that a company requires a higher standard of proof to record a gain than a loss (mostly via the treatment of accrued revenues and expenses). A more conservative firm, according to this theory, tends to opt for projects with small but certain short-term returns over those with potentially large but uncertain long-term benefits.

3 Somewhat uncomfortably for CFOs, there is a rich body of literature on this subject, including: Indjejikian, R. and Matejka, M., "CFO Fiduciary Responsibilities and Annual Bonus Incentives", *Journal of Accounting Research*, September 2009; Jiang, J., Petroni, K. and Wang, I., "CFOs and CEOs: Who have the most influence on earnings management?", *Journal of Financial Economics*, June 2010; and Kim, J., Li, Y. and Zhang, L., "CFOs versus CEOs: Equity Incentives and Crashes", *Journal of Financial Economics*, September 2011.

4 These are areas in which the responsibilities of CFOs at financial firms differ significantly from those of their colleagues at non-financial companies. Banks, for example, operate with significantly higher levels of leverage than non-financial firms; thus the cost of borrowing – from depositors, savers and the capital markets – is directly linked to the rates a bank is able to charge for loans. CFOs at non-financial firms are mindful of their cost of capital, of course, but the nature of their funding options and constraints is very different from that of financial firms, and the relationship between financing decisions and product outcomes is not as direct.

5 For a thorough account of the lessons learned from BP's pioneering role in finance outsourcing, which began back in 1991, see Lacity, M. and Willcocks, L., *Mastering High Performance BPO: Strategic F&A Partnering at BP*, LSE Outsourcing Centre Working Paper, February 2012.

Sources

ACCA and Mercer, *Generation Y: Realising the Potential*, July 2010

Booz & Co, *The CFO as Deal Maker: Thought Leaders on M&A Success*, 2008

BPM International, *Close Cycle Rankings*, 2013

CFO Europe's Working Capital Management Forum, London, May 2008

CFO Research Services, *Cash and Liquidity Management*, July 2012

Chang, X., Hilary, G., Kang, J. and Zhang, W., *Does Accounting Conservatism Impede Corporate Innovation?*, INSEAD Working Paper, September 2013

De Weerd, P., "The rise of the CFO", *FSI Magazine*, July 2007

Dichev, I., Graham, J., Harvey, C. and Rajgopal, S., "Earnings Quality: Evidence from the Field", *Journal of Accounting & Economics*, forthcoming

The Economist, CFO Summit, London, January 2013

Elkind, P., "The confessions of Andy Fastow", *Fortune*, July 2013

Ernst & Young, *The DNA of the CFO*, 2010

Ernst & Young, *Finance forte: The future of finance leadership*, 2011

GE Capital, *The strategic CFO: Charting the course for GE Capital*, 2012

Ge, W., Matsumoto, D. and Zhang, J., "Do CFOs Have Style? An Empirical Investigation of the Effect of Individual CFOs on Accounting Practices", *Contemporary Accounting Research*, Winter 2011

Hoitash, R., Hoitash, U. and Johnstone, K.M., "Internal Control Material Weaknesses and CFO Compensation", *Contemporary Accounting Research*, Autumn 2012

Kersnar, J., *The role of chief financial officers in managing innovation*, NESTA Business Briefings, August 2011

KPMG, *Global Audit Committee Survey*, January 2013

KPMG, *Who are our CFOs?*, 2011

Nolop, B., *The Essential CFO*, Wiley, 2012

Oberholzer-Gee, F. and Wulf, J., *Earnings Management from the Bottom Up: An Analysis of Managerial Incentives Below the CEO*, Harvard Business School Working Paper, August 2012

Oxford Metrica, *Reputation Review*, 2012

Quinn, M. and Stuart, A., "Not Just Bean Counters", *Wall Street Journal*, July 31st 2012

REL, "The Earnings Game", September 2012

Segarra, M., "The Glamour of a Finance Chief", *CFO.com*, July 10th 2013

Siow, R., "Erich Hunziker: Reflections on Leadership", *HQ Asia*, September 2012

Spencer Stuart, *The Global 50*, 2009

Welch, J., *Winning*, HarperCollins, 2005

4 Relationships: colleagues and partners, friends and foes

Note

1 For readers familiar with US universities, one telling difference is the educational background of CEOs and CFOs. At the largest US-listed companies, in mid-2013 Crist/Kolder Associates notes that the elite East Coast Ivy League produced more sitting CEOs than any other conference, led by Harvard. By contrast, the Midwestern, largely publicly funded Big Ten produced the most CFOs, with the University of Illinois in top position.

2 For just two examples, see Deutsche Bank, *CFO Views on the Importance and Execution of the Finance Function*, January 2006; and Deloitte, *How CFOs Can Close the Gap Between Management and Investor Views of Company Value*, November 2012.

Sources

"Peter Porrino, CFO of XL Group plc, Reflects on His First Year as CFO", *Wall Street Journal*, March 12th 2013

Banai, M. and Tulimieri, P., "The CEO and CFO – A Partnership of Equals", *Organizational Dynamics*, 2010

Bandler, J. and Burke, D., "How Hewlett-Packard lost its way", *Fortune*, May 21st 2012

Butler, T. and Quint, K., "Boards and the Expanding Role of the CFO", Businessweek.com, September 22nd 2009

CFO Research Services, *Are CFOs from Mars and CIOs from Venus?*, June 2008

CGMA, *Talent pipeline draining growth: Connecting human capital to the growth agenda*, September 2012

Crump, R., "Auditing the auditors", *Financial Director*, March 2013

Crump, R., "Spot the difference", *Financial Director*, June 2011

Deckstein, D., Hesse, M. and Tuma, T., "Peter and the Wolves: How Siemens Lost its Way", *Der Spiegel*, August 5th 2013

Der Spiegel, "Siemens CEO: 'We Need to See Calm Restored'", August 5th 2013

The Economist Intelligence Unit, *CFO perspectives: How HR can take on a bigger role in driving growth*, August 2012

Feng, M., Ge, W., Luo, S. and Shevlin, T., "Why do CFOs become involved in material accounting manipulations", *Journal of Accounting and Economics*, February 2011

Foster, LeBaron R., *Telling the Company's Financial Story*, Financial Executives Research Foundation, 1964

Freestone, R., "How to be a great finance director or CFO: three tips", *Real Business*, May 10th 2013

Graham, J., Harvey, C. and Puri, M., *Capital Allocation and Delegation of Decision-Making Authority within Firms*, NBER Working Paper, August 2011

Graham, J., Harvey, C. and Puri, M., "Managerial Attitudes and Corporate Actions", *Journal of Financial Economics*, July 2013

Guerrera, F., "Earnings Wizardry", *Wall Street Journal*, October 1st 2012

Korn/Ferry Institute, *Perspectives of a CFO Master Class*, 2010

McCann, D., "One CFO's Mantra: Operations Come First", CFO.com, October 31st 2012

McCann, D., "What Entrepreneurs, VCs Think about CFOs", CFO.com, June 11th 2013

McKinsey & Company, *Delivering large-scale IT projects on time, on budget, and on value*, October 2012

Martin Akel & Associates, *The Senior Finance Team and Corporate Purchasing Decisions*, 2011

Mayer-Schönberger, V. and Cukier, K., *Big Data*, Eamon Dolan/Houghton Mifflin Harcourt, 2013

Mergenthaler, R., Rajgopal, S. and Srinivasan, S., *CEO and CFO Career Penalties to Missing Quarterly Analysts Forecasts*, Harvard Business School Working Paper, August 2012

Monga, V., "Total S.A. Rebalancing Bank Relationships to Cut Risk", *Wall Street Journal*, October 1st 2012

Ryan, V., "Take Control of Your Bankers", *CFO*, October 2010

Stewart, D., Weiss, A. and Young, R., *Marketing Champions: Practical Strategies for Improving Marketing's Power, Influence, and Business Impact*, Wiley, 2006

Thomas, A., "A tale of two reports", *European Business Forum*, Winter 2003–04

5 Prospects: a world of possibilities

Notes

1   In the United States, until a rule forced listed firms to report
    their CFOs' compensation in 2007, a fifth of the S&P 500 did not
    disclose their finance chief's salary because the CFO was not
    among the five highest-paid executives, the reporting threshold at
    the time. CFOs are now more often than not the second highest
    paid executive, thanks mostly to their increased stature and
    responsibilities. But the pressure to keep up with peers – whose
    pay packages are now published for all to see – also explains
    at least some of the rapid ramping-up of CFO compensation in
    recent years.

2   An example is David Miller, a finance chief who left Amey, a
    UK infrastructure company, under a cloud in 2002. A change
    in accounting policy had generated an annual loss when the
    markets were expecting a profit. After Miller resigned six months
    later, he gave a spiky interview to the *Daily Telegraph*, in which
    he described dealing with changes in accounting standards as
    like "a little cup of sick and I'm not going to drink it". For good
    measure, he added, "being a public company finance director is a
    bit of a shitty job". After working at privately held firms, Miller's
    name resurfaced in 2010 as the incoming finance chief of Rok, a
    UK-listed construction company. Investor and analyst unease at
    the appointment led Rok to rescind the appointment within days.
    "It goes to show that if there's a problem with your numbers
    and you don't deal with it, you just won't work in the publicly
    quoted world again," an analyst told *Financial Director* magazine.
    "The market will ostracise you."

Sources

Accounting for Sustainability Forum, London, December 2012

Crump, R., "Interview: Former Tesco CFO and non exec Andrew
    Higginson", *Financial Director*, October 2012

Equilar, *Executives on Boards: A Profile of CFOs Serving as Independent
    Board Members*, 2013

Ernst & Young, *CFO and Beyond*, 2012

Ernst & Young, *Six growing trends in corporate sustainability*, 2012

Karaian, J., "Stepping up", *CFO Europe*, February 2009

McCann, D., "Liddell: No More CFO-ing for Me", CFO.com, June 20th 2013

McKinsey & Company, *Today's CFO: Which profile best suits your company?*, January 2013

Michael Page International, *Global CFO Barometer 2012*, August 2012

Young R., "A Merchant's Tale", *Accountancy*, June 2011

Appendix

CFO facts and figures

Form and function

Although no two finance departments are structured in the same way, a 2013 survey of North American firms gives a useful general picture of the allocation of staff in the common finance function. Accounting staff tend to form the largest group, even as CFOs push to outsource, offshore and otherwise reduce the size and cost of this function.

Allocation of personnel in the average company finance department[a]
%

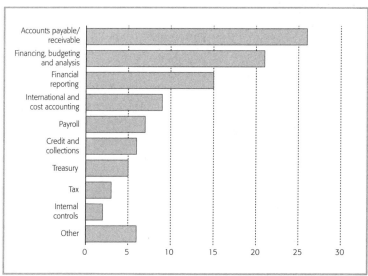

a Based on a survey of North American firms.
Sources: Financial Executives Research Foundation; Robert Half

Step by step

Companies are often conservative when it comes to hiring a CFO, particularly when an internal candidate cannot be found. Sitting CFOs are tapped the most often to become CFOs at other firms, while controllers and treasurers are the most popular internal candidates to take over a vacant top finance post.

Immediate prior position of CFOs at leading US companies[a] in 2013

%

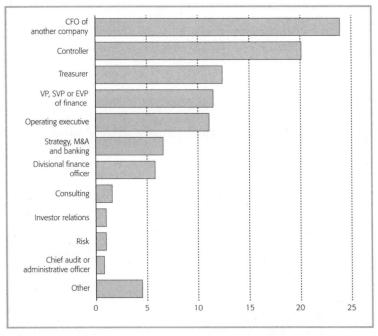

a Fortune 500 and S&P 500 (668 companies in 2013).
Source: Crist/Kolder Associates

The perfect match

In 2012, Russell Reynolds, a recruitment company, studied the backgrounds of the CFOs at Europe's 100 largest listed firms. It noticed a marked shift in the emphasis on certain characteristics in finance chiefs appointed before 2009 – prior to the global financial crisis taking root – and those appointed in the three years after. Recent hires were more likely to have relevant industry experience, a sign of conservatism. CFOs appointed recently were also more likely to have general management and corporate strategy experience, which is useful when navigating the uncertain, unstable economic conditions that followed the worst financial downturn in a generation.

Characteristics of CFOs prior to appointment at Europe's 100 largest listed firms

%

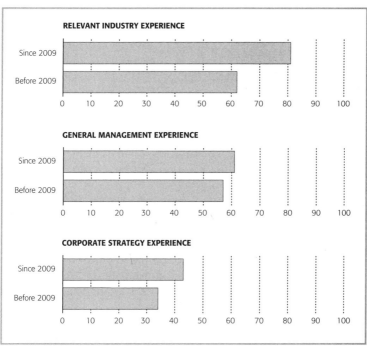

Source: Russell Reynolds

Finance factories

Alumni from a handful of "academy companies" in the United States can be found in top finance roles at a diverse range of prominent companies across the country. According to CCL Search, a recruitment company, these corporations "attract great raw talent and then help them develop to their fullest potential". Accounting firms, of course, are also important incubators of finance talent, particularly early in the career of many CFOs-to-be, but CCL reckons that "the types of experiences that are gained in a true corporate financial officer role provide better preparation for a chief financial officer in most cases".

Alumni of academy companies in CFO positions[a] at US-listed firms with revenue of at least $1 billion

Academy company	Number of CFOs	Years in role	Average revenue of current company $bn	Average market capitalisation of current company $bn	Current position in same industry %	Member of Fortune 500 %
General Electric	44	3.0	11.6	18.0	52	39
Honeywell	32	3.6	6.4	7.7	68	26
PepsiCo	29	4.0	14.6	23.3	39	64
General Motors	24	2.4	21.2	13.7	5	33

a As of March 2013.
Source: CCL Search

Pay for performance

A fixed salary forms only a small part of the pay of a top executive officer, with variable bonuses and share-based incentives comprising the bulk of compensation. Thus, the thinking goes, executive pay is linked to company performance. Chief executive officers generally receive more incentive-based compensation than chief financial officers, particularly in the United States.

Compensation mix of top executive officers
2012 median, %

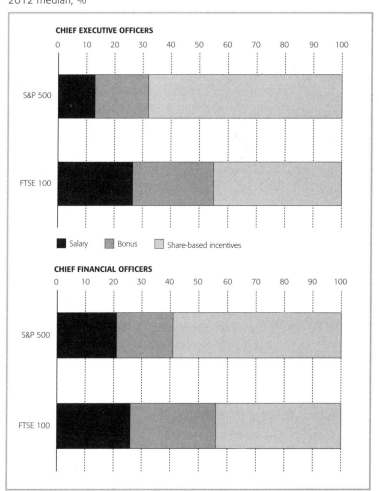

Sources: Compensation Advisory Partners; KPMG

Net worth

As the de facto second-in-command, finance chiefs are handsomely paid. At the largest listed companies, CFOs routinely make millions, if not tens of millions, of dollars per year. Large bonuses and share-based incentives make total compensation for American finance chiefs the highest by far; the highest-paid finance chiefs in the UK and Asia wouldn't even make the top 25 in the United States.

The 25 highest-paid CFOs: United States
2012

CFO	Company	Total compensation $m
Peter Oppenheimer	Apple	68.59
Safra Catz	Oracle	51.70
Patrick Pichette	Google	38.74
R. Milton Johnson	HCA Holdings	27.25
Michael Angelakis	Comcast	23.24
David Ebersman	Facebook	17.54
Stacy Smith	Intel	15.34
John Martin	Time Warner	12.62
Mark Garrett	Adobe Systems	12.59
Kriss Cloninger	Aflac	12.56
Joseph Ianniello	CBS	12.24
James Rasulo	Walt Disney	12.20
Robert Swan	EBay	11.83
David Goulden	EMC	11.58
Bruce Thompson	Bank of America	11.42
Christa Davies	Aon	11.39
Randall Weisenburger	Omnicom Group	10.57
Pat Yarrington	Chevron	10.41
Jay Horgen	Affiliated Managers Group	9.91
Thomas Freyman	Abbott Laboratories	9.66
Murray Goldberg	Regeneron Pharmaceuticals	9.62

CFO	Company	Total compensation $m
James Flaws	Corning	9.37
Gregory Hayes	United Technologies	9.23
John Stephens	AT&T	9.07
Timothy Sloan	Wells Fargo	9.01

Source: Bloomberg

The 25 highest-paid CFOs: United Kingdom
2011–12 financial year

CFO	Company	Total compensation[a] $m
Trevor Reid	Xstrata	5.03
Paul Richardson	WPP	4.18
Christopher Lucas	Barclays	4.17
Marek Jelinek	New World Resources	3.98
Richard Meddings	Standard Chartered	3.82
Byron Grote	BP	3.66
Benedict Stevens	British American Tobacco	3.49
Iain MacKay	HSBC	3.41
Kevin Parry	Schroders	3.30
Simon Henry	Shell	3.27
René Médori	Anglo American	3.12
Iain Torrens	ICAP	3.06
Kevin O'Byrne	Kingfisher	2.77
Zaure Zaurbekova	ENRC	2.71
Philip Keller	Intermediate Capital Group	2.70
Richard Pennycook	Wm Morrison Supermarkets	2.68
Bruce Van Saun	RBS	2.63
Tony Chanmugam	BT	2.57
Deirdre Mahlan	Diageo	2.46
Stacey Cartwright	Burberry	2.44

CFO	Company	Total compensation[a] $m
Philip Broadley	Old Mutual	2.44
Simon Dingemans	GlaxoSmithKline	2.39
Jean-Marc Huët	Unilever	2.38
Nicolaos Nicandrou	Prudential	2.34
Andrew Bonfield	National Grid	2.34

a Converted at average 2012 $/£ exchange rate.
Source: *Financial Director*

The 25 highest-paid CFOs: Asia-Pacific
2012

CFO	Company	Total compensation $m
Peter Allen	Westfield Group (Australia)	6.46
Frank Sixt	Hutchison Whampoa (Hong Kong)	5.87
Guy Elliot	Rio Tinto (Australia)	5.61
David Craig	Commonwealth Bank of Australia (Australia)	4.92
Terry Bowen	Wesfarmers (Australia)	4.51
Philip Coffey	Westpac Banking Corporation (Australia)	4.00
Karen Moses	Origin Energy (Australia)	3.85
Mark Joiner	National Australia Bank (Australia)	3.81
Shayne Elliott	ANZ Banking Group (Australia)	3.64
Thomas Pockett	Woolworths (Australia)	3.36
Peter Gregg	Leighton Holdings (Australia)	3.23
Kenneth Barton	Crown (Australia)	3.10
Bruce Soden	Ramsay Health Care (Australia)	3.08

CFO	Company	Total compensation $m
Chadwick Mok Cham Hung	Kingboard Chemical Holdings (Hong Kong)	2.96
John Nesbitt	Suncorp Group (Australia)	2.77
Nicholas Hawkins	Insurance Australia Group (Australia)	2.71
Yim Keung Wan	Shui On Land (China)	2.66
Nick Vrondas	Goodman Group (Australia)	2.65
Lambert Lu	SEA Holdings (Hong Kong)	2.44
Noel Meehan	Orica (Australia)	2.28
Madhu Ramachandra Rao	Shangri-La Asia (Hong Kong)	2.26
Graham Kerr	BHP Billiton (Australia)	2.23
Wei Huaning	Longfor Properties (China)	2.21
Nessa O'Sullivan	Coca-Cola Amatil (Australia)	2.16
Patrick Chan Kwok Wai	Sun Hung Kai Properties (Hong Kong)	2.09

Source: S&P Capital IQ, *CFO Innovation*

Top jobs

In general, more CFOs are being tapped to become CEOs. Certain industries are more keen than others on promoting finance chiefs, with mature, heavily regulated sectors like energy and financial services the most keen. Fast-moving, consumer-facing industries such as retail and technology are less likely to appoint former CFOs to the CEO post.

Percentage of appointments of CEOs with CFO experience at leading US companies,[a] by industry, 1999–2013

%

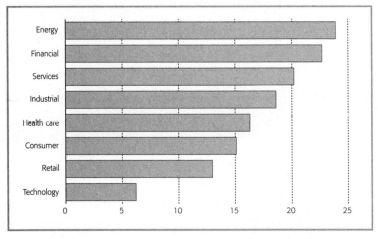

a Fortune 500 and S&P 500 (668 companies in 2013).
Source: Crist/Kolder Associates

Committee callings

Companies are keen for current and former CFOs to bring financial expertise to their boards. Nowhere is this more apparent than in appointments for the chair of the audit committee. Active or retired CFOs accounted for nearly a quarter of audit committee chairmen at S&P 500 companies in 2013, more than five times the share recorded in 2003, according to Spencer Stuart, a recruitment company. Executives from accountancy firms are also popular candidates to head audit committees, with their ranks growing fourfold over the past decade.

**Background of audit committee chairmen at
S&P 500 companies**
%

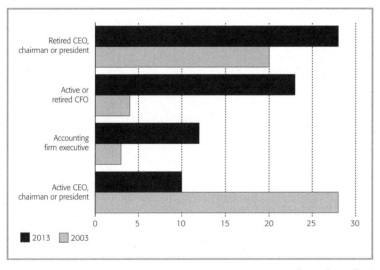

Source: Spencer Stuart

Index

PublicAffairs is a publishing house founded in 1997. It is a tribute to the standards, values, and flair of three persons who have served as mentors to countless reporters, writers, editors, and book people of all kinds, including me.

I. F. STONE, proprietor of *I. F. Stone's Weekly*, combined a commitment to the First Amendment with entrepreneurial zeal and reporting skill and became one of the great independent journalists in American history. At the age of eighty, Izzy published *The Trial of Socrates*, which was a national bestseller. He wrote the book after he taught himself ancient Greek.

BENJAMIN C. BRADLEE was for nearly thirty years the charismatic editorial leader of *The Washington Post*. It was Ben who gave the *Post* the range and courage to pursue such historic issues as Watergate. He supported his reporters with a tenacity that made them fearless and it is no accident that so many became authors of influential, best-selling books.

ROBERT L. BERNSTEIN, the chief executive of Random House for more than a quarter century, guided one of the nation's premier publishing houses. Bob was personally responsible for many books of political dissent and argument that challenged tyranny around the globe. He is also the founder and longtime chair of Human Rights Watch, one of the most respected human rights organizations in the world.

. . .

For fifty years, the banner of Public Affairs Press was carried by its owner Morris B. Schnapper, who published Gandhi, Nasser, Toynbee, Truman, and about 1,500 other authors. In 1983, Schnapper was described by *The Washington Post* as "a redoubtable gadfly." His legacy will endure in the books to come.

Peter Osnos, *Founder and Editor-at-Large*